CHEATED

HOW HEALTHCARE STOLE THE AMERICAN DREAM AND **ONLY YOU CAN TAKE IT BACK**

ALAN WIEDERHOLD

© **Copyright 2022 - All rights reserved.**

All rights reserved. No part of this guide may be reproduced, transmitted, or distributed in any form or by any means without permission in writing from the publisher except in the case of brief quotations embodied in critical articles or reviews.

Legal & Disclaimer

The content and information in this book are consistent and truthful, and it has been provided for informational, educational, and business purposes only.

ACKNOWLEDGMENTS

To my parents, Barb, and Neal, who taught me to fight for the little guy.

To my amazing wife, Rachel, thank you for letting me follow crazy dreams.

To Todd – For showing me how to tell a story that matters

To my Warrior brothers – You not only helped me find my voice, but you helped me find my purpose.

TABLE OF CONTENTS

Introduction	1
Chapter 1: Why You Have This Book in Hands	5
Chapter 2: History of Healthcare in The United States and How We Got Here	11
BUCA and the Making of an Oligopoly	18
Profit Margins of Insurance Companies	19
Why Are They Too Big to Care?	20
Chapter 3: The Pharmacy Problem and Why Drugs Are So Expensive?	23
Four Important Phases of Drug Production	24
The United States and the High Cost of Drug Prescription	26
Generic Vs. Brand-name Drugs	27
Starting Points of High Medications Prices in America	29
Clinical Effect of High Cost Drugs in America	32
Chapter 4: Hospital Charges - Marble Lobbies and Valet Parking	35
How High Charges Are Generated and Pass on To Patients	36
Marble Lobbies and Valet Charges in America's Hospital	38
ICD-10 Upcoding System and How It Influences Hospital Charges	39
Chapter 5: Doctors Don't Make House Calls, Or Do They?	43
Rebranding of the Old Ideas	48
Why Accountable Care Organization Met a Dead End	49
Chapter 6: The Broker Conundrum	53
What Roles Do Insurance Agencies Play?	54
The Unseen Players - How Brokers Are Paid	55
Broker Bonuses	56

Chapter 7: Risk isn't As Risky as You Think — 61

    The Acquisition Cost of Healthcare — 62
    Different Types of Insurance — 63
    Private Plans — 64
    Public Plans — 67
    Fully Insured or Self-Funded Insurance — 69

Chapter 8: What Can You Do About It — 73

    Top 4 C's to Creating Organizational Growth — 74
    Some Creative Ideas That Will Help You — 79
    A Glimpse into the Future — 83
    The Road Ahead: Embracing Change — 87

Conclusion — 95

Resources — 99

INTRODUCTION

"We cannot continue. Our pension costs and health care costs for our employees are going to bankrupt this city."

— MICHAEL BLOOMBERG.

Sitting outside the conference room in Raleigh, I can hear the broker and the employer on the phone with their current fully insured carrier. Anger, fear, frustration, despair, and eventually defeat. My renewal is what? Why is it so high and why can't you give me any details? I have heard this conversation so many times in my thirty-year career.

This conversation goes on for sixty minutes; before I am asked to enter the room, I have the solution, I could save this employer several hundred thousand dollars. Before speaking, the CFO looked at me in defeat and said, "You have ten minutes, our CEO is coming in two days, and we have to get this renewal down."

The broker looked at me in horror; he and I know he asked me to cancel all my meetings to fly down and help him. "I asked Alan to come down; he said he has some ideas to help us create a strategy and get us out of this mess." Ten minutes, I asked. "You might as well change your deductibles and plan designs and call it a day."

I got up to leave, still shaking my head; how could a group spending a million dollars a year just give it away so easily? They didn't even put up a fight. The broker called me a few days later, apologized for the meeting, and advised me they were renewing. The employer was going to raise the deductibles, copays out-of-pockets the employees would have to pay. By doing this, their carrier would lower their renewal from a 33% increase to 15%. "You realize they didn't lower anything; they just passed it off to their employees."

My name is Alan W Wiederhold; I'm part of a movement that believes employers are so powerful to our economy that they should experience the same flexibility, transparency, and financial security as big corporations. And that True Freedom can only come from Great Leaders taking ownership of how they spend their healthcare dollars.

To do that, we must create a new path for helping business owners discover where their money goes. We must create a model that employees will be proud of and keep more of their hard-earned money in their pockets. To do this, we tap into your Creativity… You know, the kind of creativity that makes you so excited to see your employees happy and your business growing. Getting back to the reason to be excited to be living the dreams you had for your company.

Going against the grain, I even had to create a concept I call "The 4 Cs to Organizational Growth" to show employers who were sick of 10%, 15%, and sometimes 20% rate increases. They could save that 20%, and you could lower the money flying out the door year after year. Sound crazy? You'd think so… but it's happening all the time.

So many strategies are off the beaten path that no one's even heard of before; we must do things a little outside the box. The people we serve typically don't have the money to weather the massive increases the insurance industry would like to charge, so we found a way for Business Owners, Non-Profits, Family Companies, and more to hack into solutions that are designed with them and for them.

So, we decided to take a stand. We decided to fight the status quo and the spreadsheets of ease. We wanted to take a stand for the dreams at stake when "increases" get in the way of great organizations. Large employers may have unlimited funds, but small and medium-sized businesses have families, friendships, and hearts...

We believe your benefits should too!

Unnecessary rate increases are not an option for us or those we serve; they are the last resort. So, we set out to provide thousands of employers the support they need to provide the best benefits they deserve. Thereby providing real-world solutions to keep more money in your employee's pockets.

Only by creating a true Win-Win can we seek to reach our goal.

Stop allowing yourself to be cheated!!! Get ready for a life change.

CHAPTER 1

Why You Have This Book in Hands

Before anything else, preparation is the key to success.

– Alexander Graham Bell

When I started this business three decades ago, the insurance industry was filled with health insurance companies. As a CEO and a CFO, you had a lot of options that your insurance broker could go to. We emerged from the 80/20 indemnity plans and HMOs into a "managed care system." We went from a building or "gatekeeper" who steered your care, to a $10 copay fix-anything system. The system went from a competitive landscape to a market controlled by forces beyond your control. The current system will do nothing to slow down the cost of healthcare, and if Ben Franklin were alive today, he would change his quote from "death and taxes" to include the rising cost of healthcare from all sides. Over the last thirty years, all those past carriers are gone. Each slowly died, closed its doors, or was acquired by other insurance companies, only to have its assets folded into what we have now.

Before all the acquisitions, insurance companies competed on the size and level of discounts they could negotiate with hospitals and providers and their offered services. You had options; your insurance broker had options.

Today, all insurance company network discounts and the size of their network are the same; there is no carrier differentiation.

Despite these substantial hospital discounts, what have these insurance carriers done to manage trends or stay competitive? Over my thirty-year career, I have met hundreds of CEOs who have enjoyed a growing economy and booming businesses. Many of those are now beginning to feel the pressure of the cost of healthcare to the bottom line. More and more employers are trying to figure out how to continue offering benefits and staying competitive in their markets, while employees are trying to figure out how to eat and use healthcare at the same time. So, the narrative is not the same for both.

You've been cheated by the healthcare insurance industry, which only cares about stock prices and profitability. You've been cheated by the hospitals and doctors who swore to serve and heal you. You've been cheated by the pharmacy benefits industry, where the US is 20% of the utilization and 80% of the cost. You've been cheated by a system that forces you to look at healthcare in one-year windows. But, most of all, you have cheated yourself. You have been primarily disengaged in your entire benefits process and left million-dollar decisions in the hands of those who do not understand your vision or the direction you are moving to.

Do you remember playing telephone school? It's kind of like that. Someone tells you something; you pass it down the line, and it's an entirely different message by the time it gets to you. This plays out in renewal meetings all over the country, with CEOs and CFOs only coming into the benefit decision conversation after the insurance broker has already presented the plan options from a spreadsheet. You are making million-dollar decisions from a broker and an HR professional fighting with one hand tied behind their back. Who can blame the HR professional? Most HR teams often wear so many hats they don't have time to invest in strategic thinking or creative planning.

Several years ago, I met with a government contractor in Virginia who had double-digit revenue growth for the last ten to fifteen years, with an average population of about one hundred and seventy, all under twenty-six years old.

This employer had specific behavioral health needs beyond what their fully insured plan was able to offer them. The CEO ran around with his American Express Plum card to reimburse members for copays and out-of-pocket charges. They didn't have to do anything, but this employer valued his team. This was an easy fix; we had the solution to protect them, be happy, and be more popular. It wasn't easy, but we were able to build a plan their CEO could be proud of.

Do you remember the JFK story from 1962? The US was in a Space Race to put a man on the moon. John F. Kennedy walked around the NASA Space Center, asking everyone about their jobs. There was excitement and a buzz everyone said they were all excitedly saying; we are putting a man on the moon. The legend continues that JFK walked over to a man holding a bucket and a broom.

The President says, "Hi, my name is Jack, Jack Kennedy; I'm the President." What would you say you do here? The man stood up proud and tall and said, "Well, Mr. President, I am putting a man on the moon.

How important are your employees? Are they just to fill a role, or are they part of your vision for the future? How you view them dramatically impacts how you will see your benefits strategy.

For years, employers have expected their employees to choose work over family and be accessible 24/7 while burning the candles at both ends. If the Great Resignation has shown us anything, they are done picking. Employees are saying they want both Work and Life balance.

Premium Increases jumped 47% over the last ten years. From a premium contribution standpoint, employer-sponsored health insurance plans have increased by 68% in the last ten years. Employees will no longer work under the current system. Employees can no longer afford to come to the office at $5.50 - $9.00 per gallon of gas when 50% of their salary goes to benefits, gas, and childcare.

An article in Fortune magazine said 72% of all CEOs worried about losing their jobs. After a two-year global pandemic, you are trying to find quality talent and engage them. Trying to get them into a productive setting as part of a collaborative team in a virtual environment is entirely new to all of us. We're pushing back. They're pushing back. But at the end of the day, who wins in this environment?

If you're not feeling the pain, wait; it's coming. As Jaime Dimon said, "Brace yourselves" we are on the verge of an "economic hurricane." The latest numbers from the Labor department show us the sad reality:

- Airline fares: 37.8% increase
- Gas prices: up 53%
- Meats, poultry, fish, and eggs: 14.2% increase
- Fruits and vegetables: 11.8% increase
- Electricity: 12% increase
- Utility (piped) gas service: 30.2% increase
- Household cleaning products: 9.9% increase
- The energy index alone jumped 34.6% year-over-year, its biggest increase since 2005.

So, asset prices are only falling now —things that make people feel good.

But the actual cost of living is rising—making people feel poor.

In sum, the American health care system has changed over the years. Over thirty years ago, the industry was filled with many insurance companies an employer could choose from. Today, there is a change in the narrative. You are getting less for more.

This book is written for you, the CEO and CFO; stop cheating on yourselves. Stop allowing yourselves to be cheated by the healthcare industry that is out to steal your money and snatch your American dream from you and your employees.

TAKEAWAY

- The healthcare system has changed over the years, with employer-sponsored health insurance plans at 68% in the last ten years.
- Premium Increase jumped 47% over the last ten years.
- HMOs have transitioned from a gatekeeper to fix-anything system with a copay.
- The American health insurance industry is now an oligopoly – a market controlled by few. Over a hundred insurance companies once controlled the market.
- Inflation is hovering at 9.1%

CHAPTER 2

History of Healthcare in The United States and How We Got Here

Oligopoly, plutocracy, kleptocracy: All things that are good for a shareholder.

- Jim Kramer

Health care is one of the most controversial topics in the United States. After decades of simplicity, health care has become a complicated industry with many solvable problems. For instance, the privatized health insurance system of the United States and hospitals' puzzling billing methods are part of the evolution story of the country's healthcare sector.

From the onset, the American government has always practiced capitalism in healthcare. The United States does not support a more socialistic healthcare system like other advanced nations. Instead, it has a healthcare system different from other countries like the United Kingdom, France, and Canada. Over time, the U.S. government abandoned the more global, national insurance system and went for a private employer-based system. Ensuring that only a small group of vulnerable citizens were prioritized.

A Brief History of the U.S. Healthcare Sector

Health care in the United States dates to the 1700s-1800s. Before this time, medicine in the U.S. was a "family affair." Wives and mothers cared for the sick, and only a life-threatening illness required the summoning of a medical practitioner. The practice of medicine was primitive and domestic then. There was nothing like health insurance, so individuals funded medical care from their pockets.

The idea of health insurance in the U.S. didn't come until the 1800s when a group of steel mill workers created a union offering medical protection for workers to prevent financial loss from regular spending on treating injuries. However, there were limitations and flaws to the protection provided because decisions about coverage were inconsistent, leaving the steel mill workers with poor quality medical care.

On August 14, 1935, the Social Security Act was established by President Franklin D. Roosevelt. The goal was to create a system that would benefit the elderly, victims of industrial accidents, low-income citizens, dependent mothers and children, and people with disabilities. But with the great depression, many Americans struggled with living the American dream. Getting money for necessities like food and shelter proved a real test, and many were not thinking of healthcare services. They were only thinking about how to make ends meet and survive. The state of things birthed the private health insurance agencies. However, the insurance plans available were for individual citizens, not employers.

In the 1940s, the United States was plagued by inflation caused by World War II. And to fight inflation and revive the economy, the government enacted the Stabilization Act in 1942. The design of this Act was such that it limited employers' freedom to raise wages. This resulted in employers offering workers and prospective employees health benefits as incentives instead of wages and salaries. Soon, employers in private companies were in the health insurance business.

By 1943, many employers took the initiative to make insurance plans available for their employees. In 1940, about 10% of U.S. citizens had health insurance, but the number skyrocketed to about 30% by 1946. That was the origin of the employer-sponsored health insurance that now exists today.

At this point, the employer-based health insurance system had entered the entire American healthcare sector. By 1965, when John F. Kennedy became President, he quickly made plans to reform the health care plans for retirees. Still, his plan failed after disapproval from Congress.

John Kennedy was assassinated in 1963, cutting his time short as President and making it impossible for him to effect any notable reforms in the healthcare system. However, in 1965, President Lyndon Johnson, former Vice President to President John F. Kennedy, signed the Medicare and Medicaid Act, also known as the Social Security Amendments Act.

The act was primarily for disabled citizens, retired workers, and low-income workers who were not enjoying health care benefits or health insurance plans. Through the late 1960s and early 1970s, there was another plan to reform the healthcare sector. Senator Edward Kennedy proposed a system favoring every class of Americans, including retirees.

The system was supposed to be a single-payer plan (a more universal or compulsory system) funded through taxes. But the Watergate scandal involving the administration of President Richard Nixon squashed Edward Kennedy's plan for healthcare reform. President Nixon retired after the scandal. Despite his Social Security Amendment Act, the healthcare sector faced a crisis by the decade's end. The heavy inflation and the economic recession did not help matters either.

Under President Ronald Reagan's administration (1981–1989), there was an increased push for privatizing the healthcare sector. In 1986, President Reagan's administration signed the Consolidated Omnibus Budget Reconciliation Act (COBRA). The law allowed former employees, especially retirees, to continue to enjoy the health care plans they once had. It provided a means for recently unemployed people to access private health insurance plans.

As the country is emerging from a global pandemic, the country's healthcare costs continue to increase; with reports from Health System Tracker showing over $4.1 trillion went into healthcare in 2020 alone. Up from $74.1 billion in healthcare spending from the 1970s. The trend of increased healthcare spending had existed before the COVID pandemic. For so long, the United States focused on health security without putting a check and balance on the country's health care costs. Several Acts and reforms have come into play, but none has been able to reduce the high costs of health care services. For decades, expensive healthcare services have depressed the spending power of Americans.

In 2010, President Obama planned to reform the health sector and curb the crisis in the healthcare sector by making health insurance more affordable and increasing the percentage of people with access to health insurance.

President Barack Obama worked with Senator Ted Kennedy to create a healthcare law similar to Senator Ted's single-payer plan in the early 1970s. President Obama signed the Affordable Care Act (ACA), known as Obamacare. The goal was to ensure that all Americans had a health insurance plan. So, the law made it compulsory for employers to provide health insurance for their employees.

While the ACA expanded healthcare services to many Americans, it did nothing to reduce the cost of medical care and prescription drugs. Some may even argue that ACA promoted the country's rising healthcare costs and prescription drugs.

After President Donald Trump was sworn in on January 20, 2017, Americans waited to see what would happen to their healthcare system. Before Trump became President, he was loud about repealing and replacing the Affordable Care Act. Following his inauguration, President Trump issued a direct executive order to initiate the readjustment of the Affordable Care Act (ACA). And although the Senate voted against his move, it did not stop Trump from going after the Affordable Care Act, as he resorted to systematically breaking up the ACA piece by piece. Trump administration enabled states to include work requirements in Medicaid in January 2018, which means beneficiaries of the Medicaid Act.

The Trump administration also went further to stop the payment of subsidies to insurance companies or employers. After Trump's move, many were expecting premium plans to shoot up. Insurers found a way around this through a "silver loading strategy."

The Trump administration did not stop working to reform the healthcare sector. Before the 2020 elections, there was a real push to create plans that would reduce the cost of healthcare in the country. Trump's administration issued an executive order to reduce the cost of drugs and health care and bring transparency. So, hospitals and insurers were expected to disclose facility fees, supply charges, and drug costs. And to promote transparency, the disclosed rates would be published and made public, allowing consumers to compare pricing across different providers. A competing bill was later designed to reign in the costs of prescription drugs and healthcare services. And the bill was pushed by the Speaker of the House of Representatives, Nancy Pelosi.

If passed, the Congressional Budget Office (CBO) estimated the bill's financial implications. CBO estimated that the pharmaceutical industry would lose between $500 billion to $1 trillion over ten years. The White House turned down the bill pushed by Nancy Pelosi as it was declared dead on arrival. Currently, however, both bills are still waiting to be passed into law, and the odds of that happening are very unlikely. In 2022, the cost of healthcare services is projected to increase. The Biden-led administration is working to roll back many of the reforms made by Trump's administration. President Joe Biden's office ran a campaign aggressively to change the country's healthcare system by reducing the over-reliance on private employer-sponsored health insurance. With his low approval rates, stagnation, global logistics, increase in gas prices, interest rates, the War in Ukraine, and other domestic issues, his Presidency has done little to impact the overall medical inflation.

How We Got Here

Today, the pressure on the healthcare system in the United States is greater than ever. As of 2020, life expectancy in the U.S. is seventy-seven years. This number is expected to increase with continued advancements in medicine. But since only about 91% of the population has health insurance, the pressure on the system will only keep growing. Initially, people did not like health care. They only paid what they could afford for any form of professional health services.

This means most people only visit hospitals or seek medical help in near-death situations. The reputation of hospitals was not great either, and that didn't help matters. Medical practitioners also had poor track records, so people avoided visiting the hospitals. As time progressed and medicine advanced with innovative equipment, medical care improved rapidly.

Drugs have become better, safer, and more effective. Hospitals also improved in all respect. However, the improved hospital system still didn't appeal to many people as medical costs increased and drugs became very expensive.

Health insurance was created to cover the significant health problems of individuals and ease medical care costs. Initially, insurance plans or companies did not cover doctor's appointments or preventative care. The burden was carried by the individual needing those medical services.

From the 18th to 21st centuries, the healthcare system and health insurance plans in the U.S. experienced an evolution from a simple medical system and insufficiently trained practitioners to a more complex, technological, and scientific system and well-curated insurance plans. Health insurance evolved and is now tasked with covering the ever-increasing cost of healthcare services. The Affordable Care Act brought a change by making health insurance compulsory for citizens. Insurance plans cover doctor's visits, preventative care, and major surgeries.

The United States did not wake up to an expensive and relatively unaffordable healthcare system. The country got to this state through every little decision and policy made by the government. Everything the government has ever decided to do or not do regarding the healthcare sector has landed the country in the condition it is in now. Looking at the administrative costs in the States alone, the amount of dollars spent is higher than in other First World countries. The unnecessary spending is further helped by the complex nature of the U.S. healthcare system. Another area is the rising cost of pharmaceutical drugs. Americans fork out a lot of money on pharmaceutical drugs, compared with some European countries where the government regulates drug prices. Federal government-run Medicare pays for a sizeable proportion of national drug costs. But they are not permitted to negotiate prices with drug manufacturers.

BUCA and the Making of an Oligopoly

Knowing who the best insurance company is is nearly impossible to pick. You can't tell if Cigna is the same as Humana or if Aetna is better than Blue Cross. Don't they all look the same on a spreadsheet? It's hard to know how to sort them out when you have such limited choices from which you can choose, especially when Blue Cross Blue Shield, United Healthcare, Cigna, Aetna, and Humana have dominated and monopolized the American healthcare system.

As of July 2018, BUCA stock values had increased to an average of more than 225% compared to their last five years. This is plus the fact that BUCA plans to operate in a nearly $4 trillion industry with about 150 million Americans getting their health benefits from them.

While the growing population is expected to account for 76% of the commercial health marketplace by 2025, BUCA has aligned and prepared itself for the next massive demographic that will depend on its services.

The American healthcare system, which started with hundreds of insurance companies, has gradually been reduced to five. BUCA didn't only buy the Pharmacy Benefits Managers; they also bought many of the largest Third-Party Administrators. Does that mean these five carriers have eliminated competition in the health insurance industry? Will they be able to increase the overall costs?

Profit Margins of Insurance Companies

As more Americans spend more of their income to pay for rising deductibles and premiums on their insurance, prominent insurance companies are operating at a higher profit.

As pandemic and inflation hardships are banging on the purse of some Americans, medical costs keep increasing, and making a medical decision becomes difficult.

As reported by the Kaiser Family Foundation, the cost of employer-based insurance has increased to 47% toward the end of 2011, rising above inflation and wages. That means deductibles and premiums have now taken more than half of the family income – as of 2020, it's 11.6%. According to a poll done in

December, over 46% insured adult population is struggling to pay the out-of-pocket cost, with about 29% refusing to take medicine according to prescription because of a high-cost implication. That doesn't mean they don't have health insurance. They have, yet they still can't afford to pay for the healthcare service they need.

It doesn't stop insurance firms from recording profits. For instance, United HealthCare, America's largest insurer, has consistently increased its net earnings since 2015. Now, the establishment can boast $17.7 billion as its business expands to other healthcare sectors.

In 2021, this company returned investors over $5 billion in dividends. Other insurance companies also did the same. Healthcare spending has soared high this recent year, and the American population is struggling to cope. As a result, prices set by healthcare providers such as pharmaceutical industries, doctors, and hospitals are skyrocketing even though fewer Americans have access to medical facilities and treatment during Covid-19.

Don't be surprised that administrative costs engulf more than half of healthcare spending alone.

Why Are They Too Big to Care?

Like the mortgage crisis, banks were deemed "too big to fail," Health insurers are seen as strong pillars and indicators of both the S&P and NASDAQ. As such, Health Insurance companies answer more to Wall Street than they do their own insureds. With so many tentacles into other parts of the health care system, they do not have time to police overbilling or fraudulent charges and rely on the practice of "Auto Adjudication."

The top five CEOs of Anthem, United Healthcare Group, Cigna, CVS/Aetna, and Humana earned more than $283 million in 2021 than in prior years.

"According to Pat Palmer, CEO and founder of Medical Billing Advocates of America, his organization finds errors on three out of four medical bills they review. While patients are frequently overcharged, hospitals and providers are very good about never undercharging."

Don't be surprised they don't really care. Do you know why? Simply put, you bear the brunt. So, if a corrupt medical system erroneously pays more in claims, they are not at a loss. They simply pass on to you and your members through higher monthly premiums, reduced benefits, and out-of-pocket costs.

In conclusion, the history of America's healthcare system is interesting but complicated. You tend to have policies change as the government changes. You will also notice stiff resistance from critics when they feel the plan is to overhaul America's healthcare system.

TAKEAWAY

In this chapter, you have learned the following.

- Employer-sponsored insurance started after World War II to cushion the war's effect on American citizens.
- The Internal Revenue Service made this system a business deductible expense to ensure all employed Americans could benefit.
- HMO was drafted to deal with employers who failed to comply with the rules due to inflation.
- As of 2017, approximately 170 million adults aged sixty-five and above benefit from the Medicare system.
- Americas is now monopolized and controlled by only four prominent companies, Blue Cross Blue Shield, United Healthcare, Cigna, and Aetna.
- Insurers protect their bottom line by owning the Pharmacy Benefit Managers network and don't have the time or the need to review overbilling or fraudulent claims. They just pass the cost on to you and your members.
- Carriers tout their "Auto-Adjudication," which is their ability to pay claims without anyone reviewing them.

CHAPTER 3

The Pharmacy Problem and Why Drugs Are So Expensive?

"The person who takes medicine must recover twice, once from the disease and once from the medicine."

– WILLIAM OSLER

In 2021, 55 drugs passed the FDA approval process, and 2022 is on track for the same amount. The top ten drugs approved in 2022 are expected to make a collective $26.9 billion by the middle of the decade. Have you ever wondered how drugs produced by pharmaceutical companies made it to an insurance company formulary? Do you think every drug produced surfaced in the market? Perhaps you need to understand how it works.

Facts have revealed that not all drugs designed in pharmaceutical stores or industries made it to the health market. For example, according to a study published in *The Convention*, less than 10% of new drugs produced between 2006 and 2015 made it to market. That's because several of them had to be thoroughly examined and certified not only to be effective and useful for what it's designed for but that it is not harmful.

While the Food and Drug Administration (FDA) falls under the Executive branch, it's no longer a taxpayer-funded entity. According to the 2021 FDA Fact Sheet, 45% of their budget comes from the application fees from the companies they are supposed to regulate.

The FDA also reduced the restrictions on direct-to-consumer television advertising in 1997. Leaving the United States and New Zealand as the only two countries worldwide allowing direct-to-consumer advertising.

The first trial is conducted on animals to learn how the drug reacts or works on vital organs and how dangerous it can be at different doses. Then, the second trial is conducted on humans. This involved a four-phase examination conducted through a series of clinical trials. The essence of these clinical trials is to the end that the effect of the drugs might be thoroughly examined.

Once sufficient information is gathered on a drug, government regulatory agencies such as U.S. Food and Drug Administration and others will review the drug's functionalities, benefits, and possible side effects. Only when it has been proven that the drug's essentials exceed its harms will it be allowed to surface in the health market for patient use.

Four Important Phases of Drug Production

There are four phases of drug development. That means, for any drug to be accepted in the health market and recommended for use, it must have passed through these four processes.

Now, it's time to discuss each phase in detail for better understanding.

Phase one

After some doses have been tested on animals, the next step is to gather about 80 healthy volunteers and provide information on the drug's toxicity on the doses according to animal studies. Suppose the same doses are found to be safe for humans. In that case, the drug is considered acceptable and enters another phase.

Phase Two

This stage focuses primarily on the drug's benefits. Here, the focus is to know whether it improves income or minimizes the effect of the disease it was made to cure, along with short-term safety. This stage involves having up to a hundred patients managing the disease that the drug was produced. If the drug passes the test without side effects, there is an assurance it has some benefits for the patient; then, the drug is passed to the next phase.

Typically, stage two explores a range of dosages to find a suitable dosage for the third stage or phase.

Phase Three

This is a stage where researchers are concerned with finding precise answers on whether the drug is safe and effective. Here, the number of patients to be examined varies based on target conditions and products. Still, this stage usually involves a hundred to a thousand participants.

Suppose the evidence combined from human and animal testing is found to be valuable and correct, especially if it guarantees that the new treatment is safe and effective. In that case, approval is sought from the regulatory agencies to approve it for patients' consumption.

Phase Four

This is a market-focused stage. When approval has been granted for the commercial use of a drug, phase four investigates how the patients use this drug. Again, the focus is on recognizing the drug's long-term effect on the health market, especially how patients are coping with the drug. More so, this stage deepens investigations on how the approved drug reacts in a new population, such as newborns or children.

This stage involves a broader range of patients receiving the approved drug as part of their care. In addition, every manufacturer is expected to accept the conduct of phase four research as part of the condition that must be met before drug approval can be granted.

The United States and the High Cost of Drug Prescription

The cost of prescriptions in America continues to climb. This increased cost has become a significant concern for policymakers, prescribers, payers, and patients. It has been said that 35% of every employer's health plan expense will result from prescription drug use. However, after the relatively considerable growth between 2011 and 2012, the cost of medications began to rise again. High-profile examples of very expensive new go-betweens and the sharp increases in the price of older ones are responsible for this sudden surge.

Between 2013 and 2015, the net spending on drug prescriptions skyrocketed to approximately 20% in America, outpacing the 11% forecast in overall health care costs. Now, medication prescription is an estimated 17% of total healthcare expenditures. Yet, surprisingly, this coverage only constitutes just 19% of employer-sponsored insurance benefits.

Since Medicare was enacted in 2006, the government has paid roughly 40% of the country's retail drugs' prescription expenses.

In recent years, America has spent more on prescription medications than other developed countries. For instance, in 2013, America spent $858 per person compared with an average of $400 per person for the 20 most advanced countries in the world. The price list of the 20 highest-revenue-drug costs is three times higher in the United States than in the United Kingdom.

Generic Vs. Brand-name Drugs

The main reason for increasing drug costs is the high price of branded products. This is possible because the U.S. Food and Drug Administration and U.S. Patent and Trademark Office have granted exclusive market control to brand-name companies. Although brand-name has only 10% of the drugs produced and dispensed in the United States, they account for over 70% of drug spending. For instance, the prices for popular brand-name drugs sho,t up by 164% between 2008 and 2015. This is extremely greater than the consumer price index.

The annual cost of commonly used and injectable biologic drugs such as Vimizin, Folotyn, and Soliris exceeds $250,000 per patient.

America's drug prices are soaring due to the limited number of brand-name medications that treat uncommon medical conditions known as Orphan drugs. For example, the drug for treating Gaucher's illness, Alglucerase, was $150,000 per patient when the medication entered the health market in 1991. But now, the drug is sold for $300,000 per patient, and there is a tendency for an increment due to inflation. Also, Ivacaftor, a drug used to treat cystic fibrosis, sells for $300,000 per patient annually. Both Ivacaftor and Alglucerase are received for a whole lifetime. However, medications used to treat common illnesses affecting Americans are now being sold at high costs. For instance, a new drug used to treat tumors entered the health market for $100,000. This amount is per course of therapy. While the patent for Insulin may have been sold to the University of Toronto for $1.00, he average cost of insulin has increased over 300% between 2002 and 2013.

Although the price of brand-name drugs is on the high side, another area that has captured the interest of payers and policymakers is the price of some older generic drugs. For instance, in 2015, the pharmaceutical industry produced Pyrimethamine. Pyrimethamine is a drug used to treat toxoplasmosis and, for sixty-three years, has seen an increased cost of 5500%. So, from the original price of $13.50 to today's $750, it's an almost unbearable cost for most Americans. The company could do this because it had no major competitor in the health market and lacked patient protection. Even though the costs of most generic drugs have been considered stable between 2008 and 2015, most industries have increased their price to something more than 1000%.

Another major problem for employers is the length of time a drug manufacturer holds a patent on their drugs. AbbVie's blockbuster drug Humira's patent expired worldwide in 2017. Humira's patent didn't expire in the US until 2023, which could be why Humira was the 2nd highest-grossing drug with $20 billion in sales in 2021 alone.

Starting Points of High Medications Prices in America

Undoubtedly, drugs cost more in the United States than in any other advanced country. One reason is that, unlike in other countries, the United States allows pricing between manufacturers and Pharmacy Benefit Managers (PBMs).

In other parts of the world, manufacturers offer the drug at a lower cost so that many people can access it. For instance, in Wales and England, the National Institute for Health and Care Excellence is responsible for checking and considering whether a new medication passes the cost stage. This stage has a benchmark of £20 000 and £30 000, which can be converted in dollars between ($25,000 - $40,000) per person before it is pushed for coverage by the National Health Service.

What does that really mean in the real world, though? Once a drug has gone through the FDA approval process and is ready to go to market. The manufacturer must get it from the Pharmacy Benefit Manager (PBM). The 4 largest PBMs, Caremark/CVS, ExpressScripts, Optum, and IngenioRX, are all owned by BUCA.

As previously discussed, unlike other developed countries, the US does not regulate what manufacturers charge for their drugs. The drugs are sold to distributors and pharmacies (or chains), who set their prices based on a formula. This formula is based on the Average Wholesale Price (AWP) plus a charge to fill the medication called a dispensing fee.

The reimbursement the insurance company provides is based on several factors and is quite honestly where many PBMs and their Carrier owners make their money.

Some things to know in a PBM contract are the following:

Usual and customary: The pharmacy's cash price.

Contracted rate: Is primarily used for brands and calculates several variables, including the Average Wholesale Price plus the dispensing fee.

Maximum allowable cost (MAC): Usually reserved for generics, this is the total reimbursement for any manufacturer of all things equal in strength and dose.

Because of this, pharmacies will set usual and customary, or cash, prices relatively high to ensure their price is never lower than their contracted rate or the MAC price. That's one reason prices at pharmacies can be so high.

The Murky World of Prescription Drug Rebates - Who's Really Profiting?

In our quest to uncover the hidden forces driving healthcare costs, we must focus on the often-overlooked world of prescription drug rebates. While rebates may seem helpful to save money on medications, the reality is far more complicated, with insurance companies, third-party administrators (TPAs), and health insurance brokers keeping a significant portion of the savings. This chapter delves into the murky world of prescription drug rebates. It explores how this system affects healthcare costs and access to affordable medications.

The Mechanics of Prescription Drug Rebates

Pharmaceutical manufacturers often provide rebates to insurance companies, pharmacy benefit managers (PBMs), and TPAs as an incentive to include their drugs on the formulary - the list of medications covered by a health insurance plan. Based on the drug's volume or market share, these rebates are intended to lower the overall cost of medications for patients and payers.

However, instead of passing these savings directly to consumers, insurance companies, PBMs, and TPAs may keep a significant portion of the rebates for themselves. In some cases, these entities may also receive additional payments or fees from pharmaceutical manufacturers, further complicating the financial relationships between the various stakeholders.

The Consequences for Employers and Employees

The lack of transparency and the complex web of financial relationships in the prescription drug rebate system can have severe consequences for employers and employees:

Higher drug costs:

When insurance companies, PBMs, and TPAs keep a portion of the rebates, it can result in higher out-of-pocket expenses for employees, as the total savings are not passed on to the consumers.

Formulary manipulation: The financial incentives from rebates may lead to the inclusion of more expensive drugs on the formulary, even when more cost-effective alternatives are available. This can drive up overall healthcare costs for employers and employees alike.

Limited access to medications: Due to formulary manipulation, employees may find that the most cost-effective or clinically appropriate drugs are not covered by their insurance plan, limiting their access to necessary treatments.

A Call for Greater Transparency and Reform

To address the issues surrounding prescription drug rebates, it is essential to increase transparency and implement reforms that ensure these savings are passed on to the consumers:

Full disclosure:

Insurance companies, PBMs, and TPAs should be required to disclose the full details of their rebate agreements, including the percentage of rebates retained and any additional payments or fees from pharmaceutical manufacturers.

Pass-through pricing:

Regulatory changes should be introduced to require insurance companies, PBMs, and TPAs to pass through 100% of prescription drug rebates to employers and employees, ensuring that consumers benefit from the total savings.

Elimination of perverse incentives:

The rebate system should be restructured to eliminate financial incentives that encourage the inclusion of more expensive drugs on the formulary or discourage using more cost-effective alternatives.

By shining a light on the murky world of prescription drug rebates and advocating for change, we can work together to ensure that healthcare remains accessible and affordable.

Clinical Effect of High Cost Drugs in America

The increase in the drug price in the U.S. has economic and clinical consequences. Today, every insurer has increased deductibles and higher copays for specialty medicines. Patients are expected to bear more of the cost. Sometimes, the amount is between 20% and 33% of the sum amount of the medicine price rather than making a co-payment.

Although these cost-shifting strategies have assisted payers and employers in bending the cost curve to enjoy more benefits, the system has reduced the drug's effectiveness. Almost half of 648 participants complained that they or a member of another family couldn't fill a prescription due to high cost.

Other studies revealed that most patients who opted for branded drugs have worse health issues than those who got the cost-subsidized generic drugs. Typically, drugmakers have attempted to sidestep higher co-payment by introducing coupon systems. They provide coupons that settle their out-of-pocket expenses.

In conclusion, the drug prescription system in the U.S. is why the price is soaring high almost every day; it's now more than 250% among G7 nations. Drug makers' ability to negotiate, create formidable market forces, and fend off competition is why we are experiencing increased costs in America.

TAKEAWAYS

Below is the critical information you have learned in this chapter:

- Any new drug to enter the health market must be passed through the four-phase production phases and be found safe and effective, especially regarding side effects and benefits.
- The main reason for increasing drug costs is traceable to the high price of branded products and the hidden games in the Pharmacy Benefit Management (PBM) game.
- The U.S. has the highest prescription drug prices among the G7 nations.
- Drug makers' ability to negotiate and create market forces to fend off competition is responsible for the everyday increase in prescription drug prices.

CHAPTER 4

Hospital Charges - Marble Lobbies and Valet Parking

Health care costs are on the rise because the consumers are not involved in the decision-making process. Most health care costs are covered by third parties. And therefore, the actual user of health care is not the purchaser of health care. And there's no market forces involved with health care. care.

– PRESIDENT GEORGE W. BUSH

It's no longer news that health spending in America is far more than in any other country. You have seen examples in the previous chapter. This health spending is not limited to prescription drug costs; spending time in the hospital also attracts an over-inflated number of charges.

According to Peterson-KFF findings, the cost of outpatient and inpatient care is the main reason for the gap in health expenses. To further substantiate that claim, many articles have drawn attention to the extremely expensive medical bills sent to patients, often from providers out of network. However, the actual cost of healthcare services in America is usually complicated to ascertain. This is because the healthcare cost varies according to plans across the country.

As you know, the sum of health expenses is a function of the volume of services rendered and the amount paid to providers. Recent studies have shown that nearly 80% of adults have avoided hospitals because of huge healthcare service charges. About 30% said they had to choose between paying many medical charges and necessities such as housing or food. In 2019, over 130 million people reportedly struggled to settle their medical debt.

Outrageous hospital charges also shoot up Covid-19 pandemic treatment costs. A study revealed that average charges for the pandemic patient needing inpatient attention could range from $42,486 to $74,310, depending on how complicated the matter is.

How High Charges Are Generated and Pass on To Patients

When the No Surprises Act was implemented on July 1, 2022, patients needed to know how hospitals generate high charges. This knowledge helps them to understand why they are paying much for their health despite several attempts by the government to subsidize healthcare costs for them.

According to a report, hospitals sometimes are unwilling to disclose the amount negotiated with the insurers because a list price to bargain over reimbursements doesn't reflect it. They feel it's confidential, so they are unwilling to inform patients of what was negotiated on their behalf. Despite the Act's implementation and hospital refusal to post charges, only two hospitals have been fined for failure to disclose.

However, a study conducted in 2017 revealed that hospitals collect an additional 15% from insurers for each dollar increase in list price. Hospital authorities have agreed that the goal of the charge is profitability. So, when the insurers pay more, their costs are directly passed to their employees, employers, or individual patients with increased copay, deductibles, and premiums.

Patients without insurance cannot negotiate when slammed with high or total charges. And that has been why we have seen an enormous increase in medical debt lawsuits.

"...uninsured patients were charged an average of 2.5 times more for hospital care than their insured counterparts-equivalent to three times the Medicare allowable amount.

Once a court judgment favors a hospital, they file another case against patients' properties or garnish their bank accounts or wages.

Increasingly, hospitals sell the debt to bill collectors to harass patients. If the dollar amount is small enough, the collection company will use a tactic called "parking." Parking is a tactic where the debt would stay on the report until someone went to buy a car, rent an apartment, or apply for a job. Then the member would have to call the collection company to pay it.

It would surprise you that more than 145,000 medical debt collections have been filed by hospitals in the last ten years in Maryland. Hospitals were seeking over $200 million from patients who have benefited from their services but haven't paid. It is difficult to make public data accessible in this state.

The Consumer Financial Protection Bureau Study key finds show $88 Billion in medical debt on credit records, sixty-two percent of all medical debt was less than $500

As seen in another part of society, racial differences influence patients' high charges. In 2019, African Americans were twice as likely to be uninsured, and Latinos and other ethnic races were three times as likely to be uninsured as white people.

Hospitals partner with other health care providers, such as physician staffing firms, to generate supplemental charges billed as out-of-network. While the No Surprises Act, implemented on January 1, 2022, targets emergency and non-emergency situations, hospitals still charge "facility fees" and others just for walking in the door.

I recently worked with a physician's organization in Houston to create a health plan for their employees. As we evaluated what local hospitals charged, some well-known hospitals in their area were charging between 800% - 1300% over what Medicare would pay. So, employers and members with a plan or network getting a 50% discount are forced to pay the difference with premiums, deductibles, and out-of-pocket expenses.

Marble Lobbies and Valet Charges in America's Hospital

Have you been to hospitals for medical checkup or treatment, and the bills you were given is outrageously high? If yes, you have probably been to a hospital where they charge the patient for a facility fee as soon as you are seen by a provider, whether the doctor's office was in the hospital or not. The cost of healthcare services in America is soaring high, and some underlying factors are responsible. Ordinarily, the cost of diagnosing an ailment doesn't cause more than what an average can pay for if it's common sickness.

American hospital executives understand that delivering standard services to patients doesn't start when they start from the point a doctor or nurse sees them. They know it begins when the patient steps or is taken into the hospital's front doors. That's why they provide marble lobbies and valet services to their patients.

Though some patients may arrive at the hospital by ambulance, many would come through their vehicles. And as you know, finding a parking space amid a medical emergency is an unpleasant situation a patient should not experience. Even in non-emergency instances, valet services have been proven significantly helpful to patients with mobility issues and visitors to the hospital.

Though these services enhance patients' satisfaction, it makes them pay more than necessary. Nearly all hospitals nationwide will charge you for parking in the hospital parking space.

ICD-10 Upcoding System and How It Influences Hospital Charges

Have you ever looked at a hospital and wondered what the diagnosis codes meant or how it impacts what you pay? In the medical profession, there is what is known as medical coding. In medical coding, the procedures must be reported through what is known as the CPT code. The medical code comprises ICD, modifiers, CPT, and HCPCS. These are significant aspects of coding that everyone doing it must understand first. So, ICD codes are used purposely to report diagnoses present in the CPT and in a medical report for the procedure formation.

ICD stands for International Classification of Diseases. ICD was created by epidemiologists and maintained by the World Health Organization to collect data on the reasons for deaths and global diseases. The United States is the only country that uses ICD for monetary purposes worldwide. Can you see where they could be a conflict of interest here? If I can add a modifier, I can be reimbursed at a higher amount.

This practice is known as "upcoding." Upcoding occurs when a hospital or health caregiver submits codes for more severe health issues or procedures beyond what was performed. In other words, upcoding activities happen when a doctor, nurse, or medical practitioner processes codes for more expensive or severe cases or procedures than the provider performed or diagnosed.

There is no better word to describe upcoding activities than fraud. When these activities are done, it's majorly targeted to earn more dollars from the patient than usual. Many hospitals nationwide have been found guilty of this act after prosecution. The main issue with upcoding and down coding will cause a denial of claims. It's easy to deny medical claims when they are not recorded. It's only recorded or processed claims that can be accounted for. And such procedures must be correct.

Most of the issues that occur in medical billing are caused by incorrect coding. Patients get an explanation of benefits, see some medical charges, and say, "This is damn crazy...!" No hospital is willing to give you any explanation for their charges.

How You Avoid This Error

Always read the Explanation of Benefits and ask for a copy of the bill if necessary. When in doubt, ask questions about the charges.

Despite hospitals being required to post charges for 300 of their most common procedures by July 1st. A recent Journal of Medical Associates article (JAMA) showed that of 5000 hospitals reviewed, less than 300 have complied.

TAKEAWAY

This chapter has given you a little more insight into the following:

- Hospital charges for private insurance are often 500% - 1500% higher than what Medicare allows.
- Uninsured patients lack negotiating power when they are slammed with high medical costs.
- Most hospitals don't disclose the amount they negotiated with the insurers because a list price to bargain over reimbursements from insurers doesn't reflect it.
- The high medical cost has been the leading cause of medical bill lawsuits and bankruptcies.
- The best way to rein in excess medical charges is to force transparency and share all healthcare claims.
- Upcoding issues can be addressed by a better understanding of how ICD 10 Codes, modifiers, and CPT codes work.
- Read the Explanation of Benefits (EOBs) and bills submitted.

CHAPTER 5

Doctors Don't Make House Calls, Or Do They?

"My doctor gave me six months to live, but when I couldn't pay the bill, he gave me six more."

— WALTER MATTHAU

Some decades ago, health practitioners made house calls for those needing medical attention or in an emergency. They would come directly to their patient's homes to provide care. But over the last five decades, the narrative has changed. And the leading cause is the development of hospitals across the country's nooks and crannies.

A study recently revealed that less than 14% of doctors still make constant house calls. And additionally, only a few, just 3% of those who make regular house calls make more than a house call weekly.

One of the significant reasons is burnout. During a recent checkup, I talked to my primary doctor about the lack of access, and he told me he hadn't taken a vacation in two and a half years. Doctors and Nurses in his practice were leaving their profession for smaller practices in locations that provide a more work-life balance. As he took on more patients, he confided that even he was rethinking his life choices. His biggest regret was not being able to spend more time with his family or daughter, as she had just graduated from high school and headed off to NYU.

There is a need to address the barriers to the healthcare system in the U.S., particularly the hindrance to healthcare access, which includes timely care and cost.

Long wait times to book an appointment with health practitioners, an increase in the elderly population, and the expensive cost of the emergency department in the U.S. are part of the reasons for the recent spike in the number of doctors who make house calls. Studies show people sixty-five years and above will make up 20% of the population by the end of 2030.

By 2040, the population will double and rise above seventy million. This means America will have more older adults than it used to have. While many of these people can get treated in the hospital, some will be home-bound. Some will be confined or put on assisted living equipment. And because of that, they would be a reason to seek the healthcare system performed at the patent's house. In addition, many of these older adults might suffer mobility issues that will make it unable for them to visit a doctor's office.

Do Insurance Companies offer Better Reimbursement for Physicians?

For years doctors negotiated separately for discounts with insurance companies and their networks. Remember how we talked about the size of the insurance carrier network and the level of discounts a doctor needed to take to be part of the carrier network? Today doctors are owned by large Physician-Owned

Organizations or Private equity companies. Instead of negotiating by themselves, doctors are now negotiating with insurance companies with hundreds of physicians in their organizations, giving them tremendous negotiating power.

For providers and insurance companies to find common ground on the level of discounts given and for quicker reimbursements, doctors require a no-audit clause in their provider contracts.

A no-audit clause allows the provider to reimburse the carrier for anything submitted. Since insurance companies were not in the examining room, the claims submitted were paid. Leaving many opportunities for the same upcoding and billing problems that we see from their hospital counterparts.

One of the most common overbilling procedures is straightforward preventative exams. My wife happened to be speaking with her doctor during her routine visit and asked if she had any other questions or concerns. My wife then had a rash on her arm and asked the doctor to look at it, at which point my wife received a $200 office visit for follow-up. Another common abuse is routine well-childcare (ICD-10 Z00.129 and the CPT code is 99382).

Why do Insurance Companies that offer healthcare services continue to grow?

Over a decade ago, private equity companies like KKR (which acquired Envision Healthcare in 2018) and Blackstone racked up billions in dollars as profits by investing in staffing firms like TeamHealth. As a result, this company and envision alone make up over 30% of the national staffing system for emergency health practitioners.

Their target is not narrowed to emergency medicine only. These companies have extended their tentacles to other commonly outsourced areas, such as anesthesiology and radiology. While the last decades have been known for the growing interest in private equity home healthcare systems, nursing homes, and hospital consolidation, other smaller private specialties like urology, orthopedic, dermatology, and ophthalmology are also rising beyond limitation. For instance, as of 2019, over 150 dermatology practices were bought by private equity-sponsored management groups. That was according to a study conducted in JAMA Dermatology. Practices that require expensive technology, such as dermatology, are available for private company buyouts.

A recent study reveals that the estimated annual values for healthcare services acquired by private equity climbed high from about $42 billion in 2010 to $120 billion in 2019. Nine years of huge difference. That's not the end, anyways. The rate is predicted to increase in years to come rapidly. More reasons why Blackstone, KKR, and other notable private equity companies moved into healthcare. They joined The Carlyle Group and Apollo Global Management to maximize the considerable revenue in the industry.

It's hotly debated among healthcare providers, companies, and stakeholders if the private equity system is "best" for healthcare practices and systems. Not only because it is centered around amassing wealth, but many also want to know if the model can strengthen or revive struggling healthcare investments. Profit over patient relationships erodes and will only drive patients to pay more than necessary.

Effect on Emergency Health

For health observers and experts, the purchasing of EMS by TeamHealth has caused a steady decline in the number of doctors operating in the emergency department. Significant cuts happened to doctors' resources, benefits, and compensation.

At What Cost?

You have probably seen that this private equity-based model is not the best for the patients. Doctors who try to voice out against these models might get fired without cause. Ming Lin, MD, was fired from the emergency department because he used social media to register his opinion or grievances.

Another instance is the case of Robert McNamara; private equity-based employers don't care about firing any physicians with or without reason. Robert chairs the emergency department at Temple University. He further affirmed that private equity-based companies are unreliable, as they are not shy to terminate the contract with any physician.

"It's been a disaster" is how emergency room physician Dr. Jessica Smith describes her department after TeamHealth acquired it.

According to the Private Equity Healthcare report, "Private equity funds, by design, are focused on short-term revenue generation and consolidation, not on patients' care and long-term wellbeing. This, in turn, leads to pressure to prioritize revenue over the quality of care, and overburden health care companies."

Rebranding of the Old Ideas

What difference do Accountable Care Organizations make? Do they really cut costs or the packaging of the old structure? The "managed" care system makes no difference at that.

Some fifty years ago, the U.S. Congress sat and endorsed an approach called "managed care" to lessen the healthcare cost in the country. They took this step based on the assumption that Americans pay higher healthcare charges than other wealthy countries because doctors call for services patients don't need. So, the possible solution was to manage doctors and give them financial compensation to match the cut services.

But unfortunately, this "managed" care system has no significant impact on the healthcare delivery system in the country. It has failed to cut costs and added nothing to the inflation by encouraging mergers that shoot up administrative charges.

The ACO idea became part of healthcare policy meant to address the surging healthcare cost in the US. This policy was a test run between 2005 and 2010 in the Physician Group Practice. As of 2009, it was already glaring the concept would yield anything positive. So, Congress added provisions to the ACA mandating the Centers for Medicaid and Medicare Services to include accountable care organizations in the U.S. Medicaid policy.

Accountable care organizations are clinics that partner with insurance companies to provide quality services to people to make money. Though they were primarily made to share the financial burden and risk with the patients, the system is not working well today. Primarily, ACOs are meant to split profits with the Centers for Medicaid and Medicare Services if profits are generated and share losses if they come out. So, they are basically to share both losses and gains. CMS aims to set a target for ACO at the beginning of each year. In some arrangements, an ACO that exceeds the set pay targets pays the penalty directly to the CMS—showing how ACOs are answerable to CMS, especially regarding targets.

ACO would have been the best model for a nation with lesser cases of chronic diseases, such as Medicare enrollees. So, suppose the policy is ineffective in helping patients reduce the healthcare cost implication. In that case, it is not working for the whole country.

Why Accountable Care Organization Met a Dead End

There are two main reasons why this program failed. First, the prescription was wrong, and the diagnosis was also bad. This program's underlying factor is Americans paying more than necessary for healthcare. Something beyond what is obtainable in most wealthy nations. More so, Americans get too many health bills from the fee-for-service policy used for doctors' remuneration. This system incentivizes doctors to do more procedures and order more tests. This is something that captures the will and interests of doctors. Doctors prefer fee-for-service compensation, which is wrong. For the last twenty years, numerous research works have revealed that overuse of health care is not the reason for daily increases in health costs. Per capita health charges in America are incredibly high compared to other countries because the prices at which drugs and medical services are rendered are too excessive.

Many people would wonder why the healthcare system in America is so high. It is because policymakers gave those who offer medical care services and drugs the power to control the influence of the price as they wished. And the massive cost of administering a quality healthcare system motivates sellers to increase the price at will. The excessive administration charge is now estimated at 15% of the country's total $4 trillion spent on health annually. That means the country is spending more than $2 000 per person annually on healthcare alone.

Accountable care organization was never a solution. It failed not only because it addressed the wrong issue, which is overuse rather than inefficiency and excessive prices, but also because these organizations don't have clear objectives. Or, let's say their goals were not clearly defined from the beginning. It's good to discover a problem, but it is better to understand it. Once an issue is detected and the reason is clearly known, it becomes easy to devise a viable solution. But unfortunately, from its inception at the Medicare Payment Advisory Commission meeting in November 2006, an accountable care organization has been seen and defined only in terms of its aspirations.

Another reason why this program could not stand was that it rested on the wrong premise. Everyone works for money, and doctors are not exempted. That means they work to get paid as well. So, they can be induced to stop making unnecessary financial demands if they can render their services and get paid. But we may tend to believe that not all doctors earn money. Some are motivated to work to provide quality healthcare delivery, solve complex situations, and be glad when their patient's health is restored. Worse, accountable care organizations' monetary compensation and rewards undermine those who work to earn.

A wrong evidence-free prescription and wrong diagnosis are twin defects that have affected the managed care system since it was endorsed in the 1970s. The general adoption of the cost-containment policy engineered by those agencies was the leading cause of the increase in drugs and medical service expenses in the 80s.

Managed care and other health reformation policies like accountable care organizations fail and have backfired, causing more than reasonable, creating more, and expanding the problem. Yet, at the same time, they were supposed to solve them.

In conclusion, there is no other time than to abandon managed care system. Instead, America should adopt a healthcare system that gives room for the singer-payer system, uniform benefits, price controls, and universal coverage. Other countries across the world are doing it, and they are making headway in it. And does not negatively affect the quality of health care services they render. Instead, it has promoted and added value to their healthcare structure. At least both the patients and healthcare providers will not feel cheated.

TAKEAWAY

Reading this chapter has made you understand all, but not limited to, the following.

- House-call health practices were a common medical practice in America until some five decades ago when treatment in a hospital was the new normal.
- A recent study revealed that about 14% of doctors still practice house calls, but only 3% regularly.
- Many insurance companies have expanded their tentacles beyond emergency medicine. They have now brought in other outsourced specialties, such as anesthesiology and radiology.
- The private equity-based system affects both the doctors and the patients.
- Both managed care, and accountable care organizations are a rebranding of old ideas. There is absolutely nothing new.
- ACOs and CMS are meant to share both profits and losses. They share profit when there is and share loss when there is loss.
- While it is the work of CMS to set annual targets, it is essentially the work of ACOs to adhere to and ensure they don't exceed to avoid penalties.
- Wrong evidence-free prescription and wrong diagnosis are twin defects that affect "managed" care and accountable care organization.

CHAPTER 6

The Broker Conundrum

"Insurance business is about promises and trust. It is about delivering to the customer in times of need. If this cannot be imbibed in a professional, neither he nor the industry will succeed."

— Tapan Singhel

According to zippia.com, 138,682 licensed health insurance brokers are in the US. All are selling the same five insurance carriers; there are not many options for them to go to. As insurance companies have disappeared, brokers have been reduced to a commodity focusing on service, spreadsheets, and human resource tools.

In fact, I was sitting in one of the top ten consulting houses in Houston, TX, waiting to begin a presentation. They were just wrapping up training with a company they partnered with in India. This consulting house would shop the insurance market and then send all the quotes and proposals to India. They would be entered into a spreadsheet to present to their employers and prospects. Just think your healthcare strategy is packaged and assembled like a part on the assembly line.

In 2022, the Mergers and Acquisitions within private insurance firms have soared higher than we could imagine. Many are wondering what could be responsible for this driving shift. But when you look at the need to be able to cross-sell existing books of business, it only makes fiscal sense.

Another drive is the urgent need to go digital because of the Covid-19 pandemic and increased competition among larger firms. Based on the report made available MarshBerry, the activity was so hectic that over 705 deals were brought to the public domain in 2020. This was different from the 648 deals we had in 2019. And of those transactions, fifty-seven agencies carried out two or more transactions in 2020 compared to the 49 agencies that took part in the previous year. In the same period, the number of firms engaged in the transactions reduced from 202 to 169

What Roles Do Insurance Agencies Play?

One can say that traditional agencies are the main drivers of this wave of consolidation. This is because, at the top level, private equity is actively controlling the market by investing in companies giving deeper resources, and helping to create succession planning.

As more prominent investment firms take over and create mammoth agencies, they look for ways to create efficiencies and reduce overhead. Several of the largest brokerage firms in the US have moved all their prospecting data entry to outside countries where labor is less costly.

Another motivating factor is the need for firms to have a more solid and balanced commercial and individual lines portfolio. This is needed because private insurance is a natural fit for brokers to work with the agent they trust, especially considering the complexity of customers' needs. But the best way they could have achieved that is through personal insurance.

The Unseen Players - How Health Insurance Brokers Are Paid by Insurance Companies

In the complex world of healthcare, many unseen players play a pivotal role in shaping the insurance landscape. One such player, often hidden from sight, is the health insurance broker compensation. While insurance brokers may be a helpful resource for employers navigating the complicated insurance market, their compensation structure can significantly impact the quality and cost of the plans they recommend.

Understanding the Broker-Insurance Company Relationship

At first glance, it may seem that health insurance brokers work solely for the benefit of their clients – the employers seeking insurance plans for their employees. However, the truth is that insurance companies often incentivize brokers through commissions and bonuses, which can influence their recommendations.

The Compensation Structure

Insurance brokers are compensated in various ways, with the most common method being a commission based on the total premium paid by the employer. This percentage-based commission creates a conflict of interest. Brokers may be more inclined to recommend higher-priced plans to increase their earnings. In addition to these commissions, brokers may receive bonuses or rewards from insurance companies for meeting specific sales targets or selling particular plans.

The Impact on Employers and Employees

As a result of this compensation structure, brokers may not always recommend the most cost-effective or suitable plans for employers and their employees. Instead, they may be swayed by the financial incentives offered by insurance companies, leading to increased healthcare costs and less comprehensive coverage for the employees.

This hidden aspect of the healthcare system can contribute to the ever-increasing healthcare costs, making it even more difficult for businesses to provide their employees with affordable and high-quality insurance plans. Moreover, it adds another layer of complexity to the already convoluted healthcare system, making it more challenging for employers to navigate and identify the best options for their workforce.

Broker Bonuses: The Hidden Payments

In addition to the standard commission's brokers receive from insurance carriers for selling their products, some brokers also receive hidden bonuses, often called contingent commissions, override payments, or bonus commissions. These payments are usually tied to specific performance metrics, such as sales volume, persistency (how long clients remain with a carrier), or profitability. Some common forms of hidden payments include:

Volume-based bonuses:

Brokers receive additional compensation when they meet or exceed specific sales targets, incentivizing them to place more business with a particular carrier.

Profit-sharing arrangements: Brokers receive a percentage of the underwriting profit generated by the policies they sell, motivating them to seek out approaches with higher profitability for the carrier.

Persistency bonuses:

Brokers are rewarded for retaining clients with a carrier over time, encouraging them to minimize client turnover.

The Impact on Employers and Employees

These hidden bonus payments can create conflicts of interest for brokers, potentially influencing their recommendations and driving up the cost of health insurance for employers and their employees. Some potential consequences include:

Biased Recommendations:

Brokers may prioritize their own financial interests over the needs of their clients, recommending plans that offer higher bonuses instead of the most cost-effective or suitable coverage options.

Limited Plan Options:

Brokers may be less likely to present clients with plans from carriers that do not offer lucrative bonus payments, restricting the range of options available to employers.

Increased Costs:

Hidden bonus payments can contribute to higher healthcare costs, as insurance carriers may pass the cost of these payments on to employers through increased premiums.

The Importance of Transparency

To ensure that brokers act in the best interests of their clients, transparency in the broker-client relationship is crucial. Employers should be aware of the compensation structure for their broker, including any hidden bonus payments, and consider the following steps to promote transparency:

Request Full Disclosure:

Employers should ask brokers to disclose all forms of compensation they receive from insurance carriers, including standard commissions, bonuses, and any other financial incentives.

Review Broker Contracts:

Employers should carefully review their broker contracts to ensure that compensation arrangements align with their organization's best interests and not create conflicts of interest.

Seek Multiple Quotes:

Employers should request quotes from multiple brokers and carriers to ensure they receive the most competitive rates and coverage options.

Consider Fee-Based Brokers:

Employers may explore working with fee-based brokers, who charge a flat fee for their services rather than receiving commissions and bonuses from insurance carriers. This can help minimize potential conflicts of interest.

The New System

As you are starting to see, the current health insurance sales process is like a real estate agent representing both the buyer and a seller in a home sale. They don't expect the seller's agent to give the buyers the lowest price or provide a vivid explanation of the unnecessary costs that add weight to the sales.

As you have read, the average employer-based health insurance premiums have increased in the last two decades. We are talking about how it has tripled and raised $20,000 for a family of four. The more significant challenge is fighting the broker and producer complacency and mistrust of emerging new ideas.

Think about your renewal and ask yourself these questions:

Am I buying my healthcare strategy the same way I want our product positioned in the marketplace?

Is my broker bringing me a multiple-year strategy or a one-year spreadsheet?

Are they coming in alone or collaborating with their partners to bring me a solution that will address my needs and specific trends?

It is difficult to fight a system because insurance companies have made it easy for brokers and producers to sell their products. Still, if you have asked these questions honestly and do not like the answer, you may have to make some changes.

TAKEAWAY

- In this chapter, you have made to know the following.
- M&A within private insurance firms has soared high because of a lack of market innovation.
- Most insurance brokers sell services, spreadsheets, and payroll/HR systems.
- Who is paying your broker, you or the carrier, and what are you getting for it?
- Brokers' bonuses can shoot up to $100,000 per group; no amount is too high as charges.

CHAPTER 7

Risk isn't As Risky as You Think

"Risk comes from not knowing what you're doing."

– WARREN BUFFETT

It doesn't matter whether you're fully insured or self-funding. The premiums you pay are the same; the only difference is that fully insured carriers are better at hiding where the money goes.

Every year you will go through the same renewal process. Your renewal meeting is just the beginning of the negotiation process with your current carrier. The insurance company renewal will always be higher than needed. The carrier wants to make sure they make as much money as possible while insulating themselves from you, cutting into their profit margins in the future. You will be given a spreadsheet of alternative carriers and plan designs.

While they all look similar, none of these plans will be tailored to you or your company's goals. There is no such thing as a bad risk, only informed risk. You can do three things with risk: retain, reduce, or transfer. You have transferred all the control and opportunity to save by transferring all the risk. No insurance plan can cure cancer or protect your members from the day-to-day catastrophic things in a health plan. But when you hear that one strategy is riskier, you should understand that nothing worthwhile is free. Each plan, however, has levelers that lower your risk.

The Acquisition Cost of Healthcare

I'd like to provide a brief overview of the expense of healthcare in case you still need convincing on why you should make that decision. When the demand exceeds the supply, healthcare becomes pricey. The patient, the hospital/physician/drug companies, the insurer, and the employer bear some financial burdens of healthcare costs in populated areas like the US. Three categories of healthcare expenses can be identified: intangible, direct, and indirect costs.

Often, we only think about the transactional side of healthcare; unfortunately, when a member interacts with the system, it's because something happened in their lives. According to Finkelstein and Corso, 2003; Gold et al., 1996, **Indirect costs** encompass missed wages for the patient and his or her caregivers and other possible opportunity costs. This is undoubtedly impacted by the patient's age, social support position, and other factors, in addition to the severity and length of their illness. Cancer is the best example of this. The first five words after a Cancer diagnosis are, "I Have Cancer. Now What."

Direct costs are the expenses that are directly connected to the cost of care or prescriptions written. The cost of care in Brown County, Indiana, will be monumentally different than that in New York, San Francisco, or larger metropolitan cities. While we discuss the role of Medicare as an insurer, some hospitals charge seven to eighteen times more than Medicare, ultimately affecting your premiums. You have no control over how these prices are set. Most fully insured carriers will not allow you to drill down enough to evaluate.

Intangible costs include the monetary worth of misery, fear, worry, and societal costs. However, they are rarely used as outcomes in clinical research studies because they are challenging to evaluate.

Healthcare costs have risen dramatically for many reasons an increasing population, increase healthcare utilization, changes in the prevalence or incidence of diseases, and increases in the price and volume of services.

Having recognized the factors accelerating health care and the component of healthcare cost, the next item to be examined is the types of health insurance plans. This knowledge will help you navigate insurance plans aligned with your income and need.

Different Types of Insurance

Health insurance comes in different dimensions suited to your need, according to your preference or income. You don't have to be told the importance of health insurance, so even if your finances are tight, minimum insurance is an option. For instance, you could be one of the eighty million Americans who qualify for Medicaid if your income is modest. Also, you can qualify for subsidized coverage under the federal Affordable Care Act if your income is reasonable yet doesn't allow you to afford insurance coverage.

You can also sign up for an insurance plan if your company offers workplace insurance. It is usually the best and least costly choice for workers. According to Kaiser Family Foundation's research, the estimated yearly premium cost to the worker in an employer-sponsored healthcare program in 2021 was $22,221 for a family plan and $7,739 for single coverage.

Health insurance can either be private or public. The government sponsors the public one. At the same time, the corporate bodies own the private ones. They are divided into different types, which will be explained in the following sections.

Private Plans

Health Maintenance Organizations (HMOs)

It provides a constrained selection of healthcare providers but also has lower copayments and covers more preventative care. They are evaluated and approved by the National Committee for Quality Assurance. This plan has the least amount of paperwork compared to other options. For the care to be covered by the health plan, you need a primary care physician to oversee your care and refer you to specialists as required; most HMOs will require a reference before you may see a specialist.

Under this plan, you should see a doctor within your network. Failure to comply with this will make you responsible for paying the entire cost if you see a physician not covered by the network. In addition, emergency services/treatments must be reimbursed at in-network charges.

How it works

- You pay a premium each month to obtain insurance.
- **Deductible:** Your plan may ask you to pay the specified sum before receiving care other than for preventative care.
- For each type of care, there may be copays or coinsurance. These fees differ according to your plan and contribute to your deductible. A copay is a set amount,

often $15, that you must pay at the time of service. Coinsurance is when you pay a percentage of the costs associated with your care, for instance, 20%.

Preferred Provider Organizations (PPOs)

Unlike HMOs, they provide more options when choosing a provider because they supply you with a list of them. Also, a primary care physician is not required to recommend you to a specialist. However, they are like the first plan in terms of cost and network system; they also offer lesser copayments. There are higher out-of-pocket expenses if you see doctors who are not in your insurance network as opposed to those who are.

You will be expected to fill paper works if you see a doctor out-network with the PPO. Conversely, there is little to no paperwork if it is within the network with the PPO. Therefore, you must pay the provider if you utilize an out-of-network service. Afterward, you must submit a claim for the PPO plan to reimburse you.

How it works:

- You are to pay a premium which is the amount you pay for insurance each month.
- **Deductible:** There may be a deductible for some PPOs. However, your deductible will likely increase if you see a doctor not in your insurance network.
- **Coinsurance or Copay**: When you receive care, you must pay a copay, usually a fixed price of $15. Coinsurance is when you pay a percentage of the costs associated with your care, for instance, 20%.

Exclusive Provider Organization (EPO)

Regions with a strong interest in HMO presence may want to consider one possible solution; an in-network-only place called an EPO. Like the PPO, it offers more flexibility than a traditional HMO. But because there is no out-of-network you, unless of an emergency. You can contact any doctor within your EPO's network. The cost is reduced compared to a PPO provided by the same insurer. With an EPO, there is minimal paperwork to documentation.

How it works:

- An amount called a premium will be required of you.
- Deductible: Deductible could exist for some EPOs.
- Copay or coinsurance: A copay is a set payment made when care is received, usually $15. Coinsurance is when you pay a percentage of the costs associated with your care, for instance, 20%.

Point-of-Service Plan (POS)

It incorporates the features of PPO with HMO. It operates at a lower rate than the HMO. However, the provider network is smaller than the PPO plan. Like the PPO plan, POS plans also require choosing a primary care provider (PCP) from the plan's network of primary care specialists and doctors. Your selected PCP serves as a home base for care and advice. Thus, your needs become easily known, which helps you get more coordinated health care.

As in other plans, if you see a doctor outside the POS plan's network, you will have extra costs to cover, leaving more responsibility than imagined. You will also be held responsible for filing any claims yourself. In addition, if you go out of network, you must sponsor your medical bill. Afterward, you can submit a claim to your POS plan to pay you back.

How it works:

- You will be required to pay an amount known as the monthly premium for insurance.
- Deductible: Depending on your plan, you may be required to pay the amount of a deductible before it covers your care beyond preventive services. Also, you might be expected to pay a higher deductible if you see an out-of-network provider.
- Coinsurance or copays: A copay is usually charged at $15. It is the payment made when you get care or coinsurance, which is a percent of the care costs. However, these payments' costs increase when you use an out-of-network doctor.

Public Plans

The government has narrowed down its care for a particular segment due to existing plans and support from private plans. The parts of society eligible for these care services are the elderly, the disabled, and the poor. However, these programs differ and have specific kinds of people to whom they are subject.

Medicare

The establishment of Medicare as a national health insurance program date back to 1966. It provides health insurance for the elderly and younger people with various disabilities and end-stage renal disease, ALS. Medicare provided almost 60 million individuals with healthcare in the US, over 51 million of which were older than 65 in 2018.

The Medicare program is broken into **four** parts:

Hospitals, hospice care, and skilled nursing are included under **Part A**.

Part B: This section contains outpatient services, which include certain providers' services while a patient is at a hospital, and outpatient hospital expenses.

Part C is an option that allows consumers to select health plans that offer at least the same service coverage as Parts A and B, frequently the benefits of Part D, and an annual out-of-pocket spending cap that Parts A and B do not. Parts A and B must be signed to sign this section. It is also called Managed Medicare.

Most self-administered prescription medications are covered under **Part D.**

Medicaid

It has been statistically proven that Medicaid is the most significant funding source for health and medical services for people with limited income in the United States. It is estimated that Data shows that 71 million people with low income or disabilities, covering about 23% of the total US population, are being provided with health insurance in the US. It is a state and federal program that helps people with low income and resources to pay medical fees while covering benefits generally not covered by Medicare, such as personal care services and nursing home care.

The Affordable Care Act

The Affordable Care Act was signed into law by ex-president Barack Obama. Health insurance was made mandatory for everyone in the Act. Low-income earners were made provision for through taxing healthcare providers and high-income families. In addition, there was a reduction in healthcare costs, and poor people got treatments for chronic illnesses without using the emergency room.

Child Health Insurance Program

It is a program designed to cover health insurance for children of families with an average income not low enough to qualify for Medicaid. It was initially called the State Children's Health Insurance Program (SCHIP).

Fully Insured or Self-Funded Insurance

Companies that provide insurance plans for their employees usually have two options: fully insured and self-funded. The two are both driven by the common goal of giving health insurance benefits to the workers. However, some are in a dilemma about which type of funding to leverage because of the seemingly complicated terms and packages. Are you looking for an insurance plan for your employees? If you answered yes, you need to get familiar with the basics of the two types of plan funding before just picking one.

Fully Insured Health Plan

A fully insured health plan is acquired when an employer or organization receives health insurance from a commercial insurer on behalf of its workers or association members. The employer pays the monthly insurer premiums in return for the insurer taking on the financial risk associated with administering and providing coverage under the plan. Some of these are passed on to the employees using payroll deductions. Any medical claims filed by employees must be paid for by the insurance, not the employer (as opposed to a self-insured health plan, in which the employer covers the bills).

Employers who choose a fully insured health plan over a self-insured unknowingly pay more under the perception that it's less complicated and needs no more effort from them. Fully insured health plans are subjected to state insurance requirements, and 25% of the carrier profits from the provider. The problem with this arrangement is regardless of whether you use the plan or not, you do not have the ability to receive unused premiums and no ability to be creative in what you offer.

Self-Funded Insurance Plan

In a self-insured plan, the employer covers the financial expenses for providing health care benefits to its employees. In this plan, companies pay for claims rather than paying an insurance carrier a preset amount every month (premium). To set aside money (from employee and corporate contributions) to pay out claims incurred, a self-insured company may often set up a separate bank account.

Monthly medical and Rx claims, administration fees, and reinsurance (stop loss) premiums make up self-funded coverage. In addition, self-insured health plans are subject to federal ERISA requirements rather than state insurance laws. With this plan, employers will have a much better opportunity to create a multiple-year strategy based on what's important to the employer.

Companies with a healthy workforce often prefer this arrangement to fully insured plans because of their ability to save money by only paying for the services rendered. This approach also allows the employer to bring integrated solutions to address specific high-cost trends employers may face. In addition, they have more influence over their network strategy and the design of their benefit plans since they obtain transparent access to their data. Finally, to facilitate better accountability and effective job, employers can modify their health plans using recommendations from the data.

Fully insured employers lack the same decision-making resources since commercial insurers do not permit access to their claims data. Also, a self-funded plan can navigate complex situations from high-cost claims from workers who could get cancer, require dialysis, or have premature babies. Stop-loss reduces the risk while allowing businesses with these types of patients on their plan to negotiate the stop-loss market because of the access to more carriers than the BUCA model. Stop-loss insurance leverages your financial leverage and ability to negotiate without having to disrupt doctor networks or prescription coverages.

No risk is too significant to accept since your future health depends on your current choices. This approach aligns the business model with future goals for companies looking to create a long-term culture. In addition, it demonstrates your interest in the happiness of your employees.

Employers can choose a fully insured health plan and be told what to do or a self-insured healthcare plan. The second requires the employer's full attention and supervision, allowing employers to pay what they are worth. The business can save money with healthy employees because they do not need to pay an insurer any predetermined fees. Still, employers will have many more options to reduce their claims with integrated solutions in more challenging times. Unlike those in a fully insured plan who leave the creativity and ability to manage costs to those whose only interest is profitability.

Protection Drives Production

TAKEAWAY

- Healthcare costs are increasing alarmingly due to increased costs from hospitals, providers, and specialty drugs. In the next five years, 35% of all employers' medical spending will be on prescription drugs.
- Healthcare costs can be divided into intangible, direct, and indirect costs.
- There are two types of health insurance plans: Private and Public plans.
- The government oversees the public plan, while the private one is concentrated in the hands of a few carriers.
- The two plans have their specifications. For example, public plans have a specified audience. In contrast, private plans have options related to the income of the people involved.
- Employers can opt for the fully insured health plan or the self-insured one.

CHAPTER 8

What Can You Do About It

If money is your hope for independence, you will never have it. The only real security that a man will have in this world is a reserve of knowledge, experience, and ability.

– Henry Ford

Hospitals, Doctors, Big Pharma, and brokers who only go to the same five carriers influence how healthcare is purchased and will keep your healthcare budget increasing yearly.

Hopefully, you can see you are being cheated in one way or another. Now, what is next? First, you must take a step. Now that you have noticed you have been cheated, the next thing is to admit it. Then, ask yourself what you can do about it. Remember, we've been taught we have the power to adopt or to change.

Employees have now realized what is going on, and you must understand why they are asking and remember it's not about you.

To help you stay in control, I have developed a multi-year strategy that begins with what I call the Four C's to Create Organizational Growth. Let's dive into the nitty-gritty of this structure to know how it can help you put things in order in your organization.

Top 4 C's to Creating Organizational Growth

When building a company's culture assures growth and development, you hear people talk about the 4Cs. This is a common term among investors, employees, and employers passionate about creating a change or improvement in a company with an existing structure and culture. Successful employers are mindful of this term because it is a key that drives their establishment.

However, the four Cs you will learn might differ from what you are used to. This is because these four Cs are tailored to meet and solve any problem that might arise when insuring your employees.

I am here to tell you a claim is not just a claim; never believe that. Most of the time, members interact with healthcare, not knowing what to do or where to go, spending enormous unnecessary sums of money.

Below are the four Cs you need to know:

- Clarity (of Purpose)
- Consistency (of Risk)
- Containing (Cost)
- Culture (Creating New)

Now, let's dive into these Cs to know how you can help create organizational growth.

Now, let's dive into these Cs to know how you can help create organizational growth.

Clarity (of Purpose) Why do you offer what you do?

Creating plans that have a meaningful impact on employees' health is difficult, especially when the average employee spends less than 30 minutes per year making their benefit elections.

The Great Resignation has taught us we are in an increasingly competitive environment. Not only for talent but to create a flexible health plan to meet their needs while simplifying administration and opportunities for savings.

Historically all benefits are one size fits; to remain competitive, employers must start thinking outside the box and getting creative.

Consistency (of Risk) How are you spending it, and is it the best use of your money?

Do your plans mirror your purpose, or is there misalignment? Are the current benefits in place because of too many increases, or perhaps a former HR or C-Suite member was chasing the next shiny penny? Access to high-level actionable data allows you to design a healthcare strategy that aligns with your purpose.

The more transparent your data, the more you can use it to cut waste from your plans and create programs that encourage your employees to use them based on data and a road map. Your health care plan should show your members you value their contribution to the organization by what you offer.

Containing Cost Are my members getting the best deal they can?

Everyone likes a deal, but healthcare is personal and episodic. Most employees engage in healthcare when something has already happened or is happening. If you are fully insured, there is very little you can do to contain year-over-year costs. Everything you implement only increases the insurance carrier's profit margins. The current strategy of holding your breath and hoping you get a decent renewal will get you nothing but reductions in your benefits and increases in your premiums. Engage your employees where they are by ensuring they have access to the best possible care with the most affordable options that benefit them and you. Be creative in your thinking and leave nothing off the table.

Culture (Creating New) How do we use all the tools to create a new culture in the new virtual world?

Are you using all the tools to create a new culture in the virtual world? Remember, we are emerging from a global pandemic, and our employees and families are trying to figure it all out. The Great Resignation shows that employees can and will remain at home and work. We live in a digital age that can and should accommodate that. What digital tools do you offer to keep your health plan simple, easily understandable, and affordable? While trying to figure out how to get employees back to work, it will be more important than ever to communicate, educate and advocate telephonically and virtually.

Therefore, your goals should include creating a new company culture that embraces digital tools to increase productivity and reduce costs.

Demand Transparency from Your Insurance Company

Most carriers refuse to provide data under the guise of HIPAA. Still, states such as Texas have become vital to bending the health cost without violating HIPAA. When discussing an effective way to curb increasing health costs and ensure claims transparency, you are probably debating access to actionable data.

Texas House Bill is based on Statute 1215 of the Insurance Code and applies to fully insured employer groups. It forces insurers' existing requirements to prepare adequately for employer groups with historical claims.

This new law set a new standard as it requires insurers to respond requested from a plan administrator for a report of claim information within 30 days. All the claim information is expected to have all the details of the insurer responding to the request.

Information like the total amount of claims, the sum of monthly premiums, employee census information, and monthly aggregate paid claims experience.

Most importantly, the law requires the insurer to provide individual claims reports and a separate description when paid claims exceed $15,000 within 12 months. Specific calms above that amount will require the insurer to produce additional information such as the amount paid, the individual identity, dates of services, diagnoses code, and procedures performed. None of this information violates HIPAA and should be given by every insurance carrier in every state.

What Difference Does Claim Data Make?

When brokers search for lower costs for employers, they try their best to avoid community rating proposals. One challenge with insurance carrier renewals is the house always wins. If you are fortunate to see a renewal calculation, there is always a slant on how the data is skewed.

Each year, carrier renewals can look completely different. Changing how the average trend is used, what claims were included in their calculations, how they weigh claims from this year to last, or how much to consider to the community compared to how you run on your own claims will have a dramatic effect on the amount of additional money is needed as an increase. The carrier will always show the information in the worst possible way to favor the increase required. The best way to control or keep the price in check is to have the ability to review the calculations of the claims. In other words, pricing is accurately done through claims information to help control costs.

Having access to large claims data is credibly significant. Things come up in every plan, and while some groups may exceed their expected claims, there are programs and ways to assist a member in navigating the healthcare maze that could reduce the exposure of both the employer and the member. These types of situations are referred to as a 'shock claim.'

Often, shock claims instances don't require follow-up treatment or are managed; they will be perceived much better during underwriting. When you have claims data of a particular company, you will be able to know how they used their insurance in the previous year. And that can be a determining factor in considering future costs.

A carrier has 12-24 months of continuous claims data for group rating. All you need to do is to be aware of how to access it or work with someone who does. It may cost big if you fail to request that. But when you have it alongside, some additional information can help to develop a formidable lower-cost group's claims.

Some Creative Ideas That Will Help You

Slow the Auto Adjudication Process

When an organization is trying to cut costs and save money, it starts by re-evaluating its benefits plan. Of course, they also consider many options in their search for better solutions. But when it comes to health insurance firms, you will discover that the rising costs of health care services add more pressure to that search.

One underlying factor that can negatively influence the cost of premiums is auto-adjudication. Knowing that is needful in enhancing your financial decision.

Do you Really Know what Auto-adjudication means?

BUCA loves to tout its high auto adjudication rate. Unfortunately, High Auto-adjudication leads to mismanagement of claims, higher out-of-pocket costs for your members, and higher payouts counted toward your renewal every year. According to an analysis by MHS (Medliminal Healthcare Solutions), four out of five hospital bills have errors.

If the carrier agrees to auto-adjudicate, the review process is reduced, and the claims are paid whether they are correct.

Why Would Carriers Auto-adjudicate?

When negotiations start between hospitals and carriers, the first-rate the hospital will agree to is the chargemaster price or rate. When the chargemaster rate is established, the carriers will move to convince the hospitals to reduce their costs for a better rate.

Ultimately the hospital, as we have discussed, will increase their chargemaster pricing to give the perception of a percentage of discounts. As we discussed, insurance companies are too large to examine claims. Hospitals and insurance companies are more interested in profit instead of curtailing costs.

How Employers Can Benefit from Auto-Adjudication

Slowing down the auto-adjudication process only benefits the employer and their members. Reviewing more claims and navigating members with a few of these strategies will allow you to create lower total healthcare spending.

International Pharmacy Solutions for Specialty drugs

As we have said, 35% of every employer's health care expense will be prescription drugs in the next five years. Specialty drugs are the future revenue for all manufacturers. Take a drug like Humira; Humira came off patent everywhere else in the world in 2017 and didn't come off patent in the US until 2023. Humira's price difference is $6k monthly from the UK to the US. Employers are beginning to look for other solutions to lower their Specialty costs. There are several examples, like the State of New Mexico's plan for sending patients to Mexico to purchase drugs or employers in Vermont traveling to Canada to buy theirs.

This has been considered an indictment of the entire American healthcare system. Still, it may be a viable solution for any employer who wants to stay in business and thrive.

Lower drug cost has been the motivating factor that has made many American travels to other countries for their prescriptions. Today, over 300,000 Americans travel outside the country annually. According to a U.S. survey, healthcare services are their reasons for traveling abroad. With the CARES Act's expansion with telehealth, members can access hundreds of the same direct-to-doorstep manufacturer drugs at a 40% - 60% less cost. Saving the member and the plan time and money. Purchasing drugs from another country may be a little outside of the norm. Still, ideas like these can change how members afford their medications while keeping more in an employer's pocket.

Integrating International Maintenance Rx programs

Let's imagine a system that enables employees to stay compliant with their Chronic conditions because they can afford their monthly medications. Programs like CRX allow employees to enroll voluntarily for 450 different non-temperature-controlled, non-class four narcotics.

CRX or similar programs offer a 90-day supply of Tier 2 and 3 brand maintenance medications at a price lower than the typical cost for the same drugs they receive from a pharmacy at approximately a 50% discount for the exact same drugs

High-Cost Injectables/ J-Codes Moving Them from The Hospital to Lower Care Costs

Undoubtedly, the healthcare system is increasing, and medications are a critical factor. The issue is not many patients understand what really saves cost. Increasing adherence in mild sickness is one such that may not even affect cost. However, suppose the drug prescription is relatively high. At the same time, if the visits and hospitalization rate are low, the total health care may increase. When these cases occur, using low-cost generic drugs and targeting patients with severe cases may help readjust the whole thing and move the balance to cost saving.

Take J-Code infusions such as Remicade; the cost difference in a home healthcare scenario verse a facility could be $20k to $25k every six weeks. You would never know if you had a high auto adjudication rate.

Chronic Condition Management

Most members have no idea where to go or what to do, and when they have a severe condition, they are often helpless and frustrated. Focusing on programs that assist members with their chronic conditions will provide access to education and navigation to lower frustration and minimize health or hospitalization costs. Most employers' health care spending goes to fewer people without effective health care support for managing severe cases. Only 20% of the people with employer-sponsored health benefits in America accounted for 80% of the overall spending on healthcare services.

Some employers have resorted to shifting medical costs for employees with chronic conditions because of the high-cost implication. This has been regarded as an ineffective way of handling the situation because patients will be left at the mercy of the doctors.

Telehealth and Virtual Care

Telehealth was always promoted as a "value add," a lower alternative to doctor visits due to the low promotion, lack of understanding of the benefits, and members needing direction on where to go. We saw a 40% increase in telehealth utilization during Covid due to the inaccessibility of services. Telehealth is expanding to become more specialized care. Teladoc, the largest in the space, has made acquisitions into key types of care to provide a more efficient and less costly alternative to general medicine, behavioral health, second surgical opinions, and direct primary care. It increases accessibility and reduces the cost to both members and the plan.

These methods also reduce health costs since the patient doesn't need to be hospitalized or see a doctor.

A Glimpse into the Future

Technology is catching up to healthcare and health insurance plans. The future of healthcare will focus more on emerging trends such as care navigation, bundled payments, and direct primary care, which hold the potential to revolutionize the way we access and pay for healthcare services.

Care Navigation: Guiding Patients through the Healthcare Maze

The complexity of the healthcare system can be daunting for patients, often making it difficult for them to access the appropriate care at the right time. Care navigation is an emerging approach that aims to simplify this process by providing personalized guidance and support to patients as they navigate the healthcare system. By connecting patients with the most appropriate providers and resources, care navigation can help to improve outcomes, reduce costs, and enhance the overall patient experience.

Bundled Payments: A Shift Towards Value-Based Care

The traditional fee-for-service payment model, which rewards providers based on the service volume, has been criticized for driving up healthcare costs without improving patient outcomes.

Bundled payments, also known as episode-based payments, are an alternative payment model that aims to promote value-based care by reimbursing providers based on the quality and efficiency of the care they deliver.

Under this model, providers receive a single payment for all the services required to treat a specific condition or episode of care, incentivizing them to coordinate and manage care more effectively. By aligning the financial interests of providers to improve patient outcomes, bundled payments can reduce healthcare costs and promote more efficient, patient-centered care.

Direct Primary Care: A Personalized Approach to Healthcare

Direct primary care (DPC) is a growing trend in healthcare that offers an alternative to the traditional insurance-based model. Under this model, patients pay a monthly subscription fee directly to their primary care provider for unlimited access to various primary care services, including preventive care, chronic disease management, and urgent care.

By eliminating the need for insurance billing and streamlining administrative processes, DPC can lead to significant cost savings for both patients and providers. Moreover, the DPC model fosters a stronger patient-provider relationship, allowing for more personalized and proactive care, improving health outcomes, and reducing healthcare costs.

Predictive Genetic Testing

While companies like 23 and Me created a buzz several years ago with DNA testing to identify family heritage. There is an entire Life Science field working on merging Genetic testing with early warnings and custom member-level treatment plans.

Predictive genetic testing is a type of genetic testing that identifies gene mutations or variations associated with an increased risk of developing certain diseases or conditions. It works by analyzing specific genes or genetic markers to determine if an individual is more likely to develop a disease compared to the general population. Predictive genetic testing is often used for conditions with a strong hereditary component, such as certain cancers, cardiovascular diseases, or neurological disorders.

How does it work?

Predictive genetic testing involves analyzing DNA samples, usually obtained from a blood or saliva sample, to detect the presence of gene mutations or variations that have been linked to specific diseases. The DNA is extracted from the sample, and the specific genes or markers of interest are analyzed using various laboratory techniques, such as polymerase chain reaction (PCR) or DNA sequencing. The results of the test are then interpreted by a genetic counselor or healthcare provider, who can provide guidance on the implications of the findings.

What are the positives of predictive genetic testing?

Early detection and prevention:

By identifying individuals at risk for certain diseases, healthcare providers can implement preventive measures, such as lifestyle modifications or targeted screenings, to catch diseases in their earliest stages or even prevent them altogether. Leading to improved health outcomes and a better quality of life for at-risk individuals.

Personalized treatment:

Genetic information can help healthcare providers determine the most effective treatment strategies for patients based on their unique genetic makeup. Leading to better outcomes and fewer side effects, as treatments are tailored to an individual's specific needs.

Informed decision-making:

Individuals aware of their genetic risk for certain diseases can make more informed decisions about their healthcare and lifestyle choices. For example, someone who learns they have an increased risk of developing a specific type of cancer may choose to undergo more frequent screenings or adopt healthier habits to reduce their risk.

Family planning:

Couples planning to have children can use predictive genetic testing to assess their risk of passing on genetic disorders to their offspring. This information can help them make informed decisions about family planning and prenatal testing.

Research and development:

Predictive genetic testing can contribute to a greater understanding of the genetic factors underlying various diseases, which can help researchers develop more targeted and effective therapies in the future.

Overall, the positives of predictive genetic testing lie in its potential to improve healthcare outcomes by enabling early detection, prevention, personalized treatment, and informed decision-making. However, it is important to balance these benefits with the potential ethical, psychological, and privacy concerns associated with the use of genetic information.

The Road Ahead: Embracing Change

As we look towards the future of healthcare, it is essential to embrace change and innovation, recognizing that the current system is not sustainable and requires a fundamental shift in how we access and pay for care. We can create a more efficient and patient-centered healthcare system that benefits everyone by adopting new models and approaches, such as care navigation, bundled payments, direct primary care, and the use of Predictive Genetic Testing to create individual treatment plans.

Integration of Stop loss, RX, Care Management, and Administration

We have discussed how decentralized healthcare can be if a plan is protected by reinsurance. Still, suppose the reinsurance doesn't fully integrate into the health plan administrator, your care management, or your prescription coverage. In that case, it's slightly better than staying fully insured with more data. It will lower your expenses but will do little to improve medical outcomes, assist members and create a multiple-year strategy that saves money.

Search for partners who integrate and negotiate all these components at once. Giving a reinsurance partner a complete picture of high-cost claims, expensive drug prescriptions, and diagnoses and how they will be managed and reduced has a more significant impact than just shopping each piece independently.

Many brokers and consultants will tout their ability to carve up your benefits and shop them for the "lowest cost." Still, again by not having everything integrated and working in concert, you are reducing your healthcare to a cheap commodity instead of a long-term strategy.

Harnessing the Power of AI - A Pathway to Lower Health Insurance Costs

Artificial intelligence (AI) has revolutionized numerous industries recently, with healthcare no exception.

One of the most powerful applications of AI in healthcare is predictive analytics, which uses historical data to make predictions about future health outcomes. By analyzing a patient's medical history, lifestyle factors, and genetic predispositions, AI-driven predictive analytics can identify potential health risks and recommend personalized interventions. This enables healthcare providers and insurers to proactively manage chronic conditions, reducing the likelihood of costly complications and hospitalizations and lowering insurance premiums.

Streamlining Administrative Processes

The healthcare industry is notorious for its complex and time-consuming administrative processes, which can drive up insurance costs. AI has the potential to streamline these processes, automating tasks such as claims processing, eligibility verification, and billing. By increasing efficiency and reducing human error, AI-driven automation can lead to significant cost savings for insurance companies, which can then be passed on to employers and employees through lower premiums.

Fraud Detection and Prevention

Health insurance fraud is a significant issue, with billions of dollars lost each year due to fraudulent claims and billing practices. AI can be a powerful tool in detecting and preventing fraud by analyzing vast amounts of data to identify patterns and anomalies that may indicate fraudulent activity. By reducing the prevalence of fraud, AI can help lower the overall cost of healthcare and insurance premiums.

Optimizing Network and Provider Selection

AI can also optimize provider networks and assist patients in choosing the most appropriate and cost-effective healthcare providers. By analyzing provider performance, outcomes, and cost data, AI algorithms can identify high-value providers that offer the best care at the lowest cost. This information can be used by insurers to create more cost-effective provider networks and by patients to make informed decisions about their care, ultimately leading to lower insurance costs.

Telemedicine and Remote Monitoring

AI-driven telemedicine and remote monitoring technologies are becoming increasingly popular to provide more accessible and cost-effective healthcare. By enabling patients to consult with healthcare providers remotely and using AI algorithms to monitor and analyze patient data, these technologies can help to prevent unnecessary hospital visits and reduce the overall cost of care.

The Road Ahead

While AI holds great promise for reducing health insurance costs, it is essential to recognize that successfully implementing these technologies requires collaboration and commitment from all stakeholders, including insurers, healthcare providers, regulators, and employers. By embracing AI and working together to overcome the challenges associated with its adoption, we can create a more efficient and affordable healthcare system that benefits everyone.

As we continue to explore innovative solutions to tackle the ever-increasing healthcare costs, it is vital to examine new models and approaches that challenge the status quo. Reference-based pricing (RBP) offers an alternative to traditional health insurance networks.

Reference-Based Pricing: A New Approach to Healthcare Cost Management

Reference-based pricing is a payment model where employers or insurers establish a fixed amount they are willing to pay for specific medical services, often based on a percentage of Medicare reimbursement rates. Under this model, patients are responsible for costs exceeding the established reference price. The idea behind RBP is to encourage price transparency, incentivize patients to seek cost-effective care, and, ultimately, drive down healthcare costs.

Pros of Eliminating Health Insurance Company Networks

Price Transparency:

One of the key benefits of RBP and eliminating health insurance networks is increased price transparency. This approach empowers patients to make informed decisions about their care based on the actual cost of services rather than being limited to a predefined network of providers.

Cost Savings:

Removing the health insurance networks and negotiating directly with providers, employers, and insurers can potentially achieve substantial cost savings. This can result in lower insurance premiums for employers and employees.

Increased Patient Choice:

Eliminating health insurance networks allows patients to choose their preferred providers without worrying about whether they are in-network or out-of-network, leading to greater satisfaction with their healthcare experience.

Cons of Eliminating Health Insurance Company Networks

Limited Provider Negotiation Power:

Health insurance networks often have significant bargaining power when negotiating prices with providers. By eliminating networks, employers and insurers may lose some of this leverage, potentially leading to higher healthcare costs.

Increased Financial Risk for Patients:

Under RBP, patients may be responsible for a higher portion of their medical costs if they choose a provider that charges more than the reference price. This can result in increased out-of-pocket expenses and financial risk for patients.

Administrative Complexity:

Implementing RBP and managing direct negotiations with healthcare providers can be administratively complex for employers and insurers. This may require additional resources and expertise, potentially offsetting some of the cost savings achieved through RBP.

Finding the Right Balance: Is the Juice Worth The Squeeze

While reference-based pricing and eliminating health insurance networks offer several advantages, it is essential to weigh these benefits against the potential drawbacks and consider the unique needs of each organization and its employees.

Captive Reinsurance Carriers

An increasing number of employers with limited data are exploring purchasing their reinsurance from a Captive reinsurance carrier. There are two types of Captives. Direct writers mean they are the actual guarantor of the risk. The second is what's called a Captive manager. A Captive manager can underwrite and manage stop loss on behalf of a reinsurance carrier, and they are not the carrier. Several other Captives offer different programs, including RX and other Care management solutions. Remember, Captives are nothing more than the reinsurance or stop loss that guarantees the risk.

- Captives pull a lot of smaller groups together and are put in a "Cell." Most of these groups do not have any information on their risk.
- Since there is no information about the claims of these small groups, the shadow price of the renewal doesn't give the group the best deal since they aren't underwriting the risk.
- When the Captive goes to market, they typically buy an individual stop loss deductible of $300k for the "Cell" and charge the particular member for a smaller number (for a higher cost).

To enter a captive arrangement at a shadow-priced rate, buy-in or seed money is usually 10% of the Spec premium in cash or line of credit. (between $25k and $60K)

If everyone in the "Cell" runs poorly, there is such a thing as a margin call where the Captive could ask for more money if the captive cell the group sits in needs more money.

Most Captives are more interested in writing the stop-loss policy than focusing on effectively managing the claims. They will work with any administrator who processes claims. These administrators could have no ability to manage RX, no ability to handle claims, and no reporting or long-term strategy.

As discussed, medical and prescription claim management begins with the administrator and the plan (the engine), whereby Captives only guarantee the risk payment. Nothing more... Suppose you have a horrible experience with the administrator. In that case, you must move and re-card everyone, similar to the BUCA strategy.

It's essential to understand the relationship between administrative partners and reinsurance.

In conclusion, you read about many things that can be done when you discover the high health cost strangling your business as an employer. The truth is the current system is cheating you, taking your profits. The only way your business will thrive is by acting. Whether you like it or not, the system has been designed so that you will continue to take more and more from your employees. But now that you have seen behind the curtain, the ball is in your court. You need to make concrete decisions that will help to protect your company from this system or continue to lose profits to healthcare unnecessarily.

No one likes to be cheated on; only you can stop it.

TAKEAWAY

- The Top 4Cs are an effective tool to drive organizational growth.
- When brokers search for lower costs for employers, they don't always know what they are looking at.
- When an organization tries to cut costs and save money, it starts by re-evaluating its benefits plan, not raising deductibles and premium contributions.
- Lower drug cost has been the motivating factor that has made many American travels to other countries for drug prescriptions.

CONCLUSION

Throughout this book, we have explored the numerous challenges and complexities that employers face when navigating the healthcare landscape. From the hidden bonuses paid to health insurance brokers and the costs associated with using general agents to the potential of AI in lowering health insurance expenses and the future of healthcare, it is evident that there is much to consider when procuring and managing health insurance for employees.

The American Dream has been significantly impacted by the increasing costs and inefficiencies of the healthcare system. However, with knowledge and a proactive approach, employers and CEOs can take control and play an essential role in reclaiming that dream for their employees.

As a CEO or business owner, you have the power to make a meaningful difference in the lives of your employees by taking ownership of your company's health insurance plan. To create positive change and ensure the most cost-effective and suitable healthcare coverage, consider the following actions:

Educate Yourself:

Stay informed about the trends in healthcare, including new payment models, technologies, and regulatory changes. Understanding the evolving landscape will empower you to make informed decisions and advocate for your employees' best interests.

Evaluate Your Current Health Plan:

Conduct a thorough assessment of your current health insurance plan, identifying areas for improvement and potential cost savings. Consider engaging the services of an independent consultant or broker to help you analyze your plan and provide unbiased advice.

Demand Transparency:

Insist on full disclosure of all broker compensation, including hidden bonuses and commissions, and the involvement of any general agents in your health plan. Transparent relationships with brokers and intermediaries will help prioritize your organization's best interests.

Explore Alternative Healthcare Models:

Investigate innovative healthcare models like direct primary care, reference-based pricing, Telehealth, alternate funding methods, and how you pay your broker and the Pharmacy Benefit Managers. Implementing alternative models can lead to cost savings and improved employee care.

Empower Your Employees:

Encourage your employees to take an active role in their healthcare by providing them with resources, education, and support. Promote wellness initiatives and preventive care to foster a healthy workforce and reduce healthcare costs over time.

Advocate for Change:

Use your voice and influence to advocate for positive change in the healthcare system. Join industry groups, participate in public forums, and engage with policymakers to help shape the future of healthcare, and healthcare remains attainable for all.

By taking these actions, you can demonstrate your commitment to your employees' well-being and create a healthier, more productive workforce. Together, we can work towards a future where healthcare is accessible, affordable, and sustainable, allowing employers and employees to thrive.

If you're tired of being cheated on and are ready to put profits back into your company, now is the time to take action.

Don't let hidden costs and inefficiencies drain your resources and hinder your organization's growth. By addressing the challenges in your health insurance plan and taking control of your healthcare strategy, you can create a healthier, more productive workforce while safeguarding your bottom line.

Reach out to me today, and together, we'll work on a tailored solution that meets your organization's unique needs and objectives. Let's put an end to being cheated by the healthcare system and unlock the true potential of your company.

Contact me now to get started on your journey toward a better future for your employees and your business.

Alan W. Wiederhold, GBA

info@costofdoingnothing.us
LinkedIn: @Alan_Wiederhold
Podcast: What's The Cost Of Doing Nothing
Follow me on
Instagram @cheated_book
Facebook @costofdoingnothing
Twitter @costofdoingnothing

RESOURCES

O'Brien, S. (2021, November 11). Average family premiums for employer-based health insurance have jumped 47% in the last decade, outpacing wage growth and inflation. CNBC. Retrieved June 30, 2022, from https://www.cnbc.com/2021/11/11/premiums-for-employer-health-insurance-have-jumped-47percent-in-10-years.html

Taylor, A. (2022, February 2). 72% of CEOs fear losing their jobs in 2022. Fortune. Retrieved June 30, 2022, from https://fortune.com/2022/02/02/majority-ceos-anxiety-losing-job-2022/

Son, Hugh (2022, June 1) Jamie Dimon says brace yourself for an economic hurricane. Retrieved June 30, 2022

https://www.cnbc.com/2022/06/01/jamie-dimon-says-brace-yourself-for-an-economic-hurricane-caused-by-the-fed-and-ukraine-war.html

Department of Labor, June Consumer Price Index (2022, July 18) CPI up 9.1% highest in 40 years.
https://www.bls.gov/opub/ted/2022/consumer-prices-

up-9-1-percent-over-the-year-ended-june-2022-largest-increase-in-40-years.htm

Amiah Taylor (2022) "72% of CEOs fear losing their jobs in 2022," retrieved from https://fortune.com/2022/02/02/majority-ceos-anxiety-losing-job-2022/

Paul Monica (2022) "Brace yourselves for an economic 'hurricane" retrieved from https://edition.cnn.com/2022/06/01/economy/jamie-dimon-jpmorgan-chase-economy/index.html

NPR. (2020, October 7). History Of Employer-Based Health Insurance In The U.S. Retrieved June 30, 2022, from https://choice.npr.org/index.html?origin=https://www.npr.org/2020/10/07/921287295/history-of-employer-based-health-insurance-in-the-u-s#:%7E:text=In%20the%201940s%2C%20the%20government,We%20made%20this%20tax%2Dfree

Rook, D. (2022, August 27). A Brief History of Employer-Sponsored Healthcare [From the 1930s to Now]. JP Griffin Group. Retrieved June 30, 2022, from https://www.griffinbenefits.com/blog/history-of-employer-sponsored-healthcare

Seefeldt, B. (2022, February 7). A Bump In Insurance Premiums: What It Means For 2022 And Beyond. Forbes. Retrieved June 30, 2022, from https://www.forbes.com/sites/forbesbusinesscouncil/2022/02/04/a-bump-in-insurance-premiums-what-it-means-for-2022-and-beyond/

Strautman, Alex (2021, September 30) Health Insurance Stock Surge in 2021 – 2022

Growing Population is expected to account for 76% of the commercial health marketplace.

Paloksy, Craig (201, November 10). Average Family Premiums Rose 4% This Year to Top $22,000. https://www.kff.org/health-costs/press-release/average-family-premiums-rose-4-this-year-to-top-22000/

United Health Care earnings since 2015. Wall Street Journal UHC Charts https://www.wsj.com/market-data/quotes/UNH/financials/annual/income-statement

Herman, Bob (2022, May 12) Top 5 CEOs earned more than $283 million. https://www.statnews.com/2022/05/12/health-insurance-ceos-raked-in-record-pay-during-covid/

John Hansbrough (2022) "How Common Are Medical Billing Errors?" retrieved from https://www.lblgroup.com/how-common-are-medical-billing-errors/

Adam, Ben (2022, Feb 7). The top 10 drug launches of 2022. https://www.fiercepharma.com/special-report/10-most-anticipated-drug-launches-2022

BioMed tracker (2016) "Clinical Development Success Rates 2006-2015" retrieved from https://www.bio.org/sites/default/files/legacy/bioorg/docs/Clinical%20Development%20Success%20Rates%202006-2015%20-%20BIO,%20Biomedtracker,%20Amplion%202016.pdf

Brian Newell (2022) "New study finds more than half of brand medicine spending goes to the supply chain and others," retrieved from https://catalyst.phrma.org/new-study-finds-more-than-half-of-brand-medicine-spending-goes-to-the-supply-chain-and-others?utm_campaign=2022-q1-inn-afd&utm_medium=pai_soc_pst-fbk-adf&utm_source=fbk&utm_content=clk-pol-tpv_scl-geo_std-usa-all-pai_srh_cpc-ggl-adf-BRGReportSearch-KeyStates1-fed_uns-edu-ser-lrm-soc_txt-std-vra-adf&utm_term=&gclid=CjOKCQjw_viWBhD8ARIsAH1mCd7YP1OZZGMy2__YrpPK3OZAJVsgWnw0Y722wft-LVa5H3hsheUqgywQaAoyoEALw_wcB

Kluender, Raymond (2021, July 20) et al. "Medical Debt in the US 2009-2020" Journal of American Medical Association. https://jamanetwork.com/journals/jama/article-abstract/2782187

Liz Hamel et al. I (2022) Public Opinion on Prescription Drugs and Their Prices" retrieved from https://www.kff.org/health-costs/poll-finding/public-opinion-on-prescription-drugs-and-their-prices/

Paulina Braveman and Luara Gottlieb (2022) "The Social Determinants of Health: It's Time to Consider the Causes of the Causes," retrieved from https://www.ncbi.nlm.nih.gov/pmc/articles/PMC3863696/

Dessie Otachiliska (2021) "America's underinsurance crisis in the age of Covid-19" https://blog.petrieflom.law.harvard.edu/2021/06/29/americas-underinsurance-crisis-in-the-age-of-covid-19/

Sarah L Barber, Luca Lorenzoni, and Paul Ong (2019) "Price setting and price regulation in health care Lessons for advancing Universal Health Coverage" retrieved from https://www.oecd.org/health/health-systems/oecd-who-price-setting-summary-report.pdf

Stacie B. Dusetzina, .D., Ethan Basch, MD, and Nancy L. Keating, .D., MPH (2022) "For Uninsured Cancer Patients, Outpatient Charges Can Be Costly, Putting Treatments Out Of Reach" retrieved from https://www.ncbi.nlm.nih.gov/pmc/articles/PMC4947373/

Rockeman, O. (2022, March 10). Bloomberg - Are you a robot? Bloomberg. Retrieved June 30, 2022, from https://www.bloomberg.com/tosv2.html?vid=&uuid=e8b0ad46-f8a2-11ec-afba-734c677a6342&url=L25ld3MvYXJ0aWNsZXMvMjAyMi0wMy0xMC91LXMtaW5mbGF0aW9uLWhpdHMtZnJlc2gtNDAteWVhci1oaWdoLW9mLTctOS1iZWZvcmUtmUtb2lsLXNwaWtl

Dominique Maria Bonessi (2021) "Some Marylanders Could Be Protected From Medical Debt Under New Bill" retrieved from https://www.npr.org/local/305/2021/03/29/982458707/some-marylanders-could-be-protected-from-medical-debt-under-new-bill

U.N.O (2015) "Population 2030 Demographic challenges and opportunities for sustainable development planning" retrieved from https://www.un.org/en/development/desa/population/publications/pdf/trends/Population2030.pdf

U.N.O Department of economic and social affairs (2019) "Growing at a slower pace, the world population is expected to reach 9.7 billion in 2050 and could peak at nearly 11 billion around 2100" retrieved from https://www.un.org/development/desa/en/news/population/world-population-prospects-2019.html

Mani Bhullar (2022) "Is Private Equity a Dangerous Employer?" retrieved from https://www.echemi.com/community/is-private-equity-a-dangerous-employer_mjart2203302250_218.html

Sally Tan, Kira Seiger, Peter Renehan, Arash Mostaghimi (2019) Trends in Private Equity Acquisition of Dermatology Practices in the United States" retrieved from https://pubmed.ncbi.nlm.nih.gov/31339521/

Ross A Hammond and Ruth Levine (2010) "The economic impact of obesity in the United States" retrieved from https://www.ncbi.nlm.nih.gov/pmc/articles/PMC3047996/

Oleg Bestsennyy, Michelle Chmielewski, Anne Koffel, and Amit Shah (2022) "From facility to home: How healthcare could shift by 2025," retrieved from https://www.mckinsey.com/industries/healthcare-systems-and-services/our-insights/from-facility-to-home-how-healthcare-could-shift-by-2025

Maureen Tkacik (2021) "Wall Street Is Pressing ER Docs To Fleece Patients," retrieved from https://www.levernews.com/er-organization-admits-to-the-evils-of-private-equity/

Louise Irvine (2022) "Protect the NHS: Scrap the health and care bill," retrieved from https://www.change.org/p/health-secretary-sajid-javid-protect-the-nhs-stop-the-health-and-care-bill

M. Scheffler Laura (2021) Soaring Private Equity Investment in the Healthcare sector: Consolidation accelerated, competition undermined, and patient risk" retrieved from https://publichealth.berkeley.edu/wp-content/uploads/2021/05/Private-Equity-I-Healthcare-Report-FINAL.pdf

World Health Organization (2021) Global expenditure on health; public spending on health" retrieved from https://apps.who.int/iris/bitstream/handle/10665/350560/9789240041219-eng.pdf

M&A (2022) "2022 Insurance M&A outlook" retrieving from https://www2.deloitte.com/us/en/pages/financial-services/articles/insurance-m-and-a-outlook.html

MarchBerry (2022) "Marsh Mclennan Reports Strong 2Q22 Results" retrieved from https://www.marshberry.com/resource/marsh-mclennan-reports-strong-2q22-results/

New York's EmblemHealth (2022) "46 posts categorized "Insurance" retrieved from https://ivebeen-mugged.typepad.com/my_weblog/insurance/

Olena Hankivsk and Jane Friesen (2004) "Expanding Economic Costing in Health Care: Values, Gender and Diversity" retrieved from https://www.researchgate.net/publication/4835816_Expanding_Economic_Costing_in_Health_Care_Values_Gender_and_Diversity

KFF (2021) "2021 Employer Health Benefits Survey" retrieved from https://www.kff.org/report-section/ehbs-2021-section-1-cost-of-health-insurance/

Sarah Elbeshbishi (2022) "Lack of universal health care cost 300,000 American lives in pandemic, study shows," retrieved from https://www.usatoday.com/story/news/health/2022/06/23/universal-healthcare-save-american-lives-pandemic/7652206001/?gnt-cfr=1

Nigel S.B. Rawson, PhD, and Louise Binder, LLD (2017) "Importation of drugs into the United States from Canada" retrieved from https://www.ncbi.nlm.nih.gov/pmc/articles/PMC5478407/

www.ingramcontent.com/pod-product-compliance
Lightning Source LLC
Chambersburg PA
CBHW070241220526
45465CB00004B/1473